公式 TOEIC® Listening & Reading 問題集

問題集

音声ダウンロード(無料)のご案内

下記の二次元バーコードまたは **URL** から、音声ダウンロードに関するページにアクセスし、記載の手順に従って音声ファイルをダウンロード・再生してください。

https://iibc.me/dl_audios

はじめに

　本書は『公式 TOEIC® Listening & Reading 問題集』シリーズの第11弾です。2016年5月実施の公開テストから加わった出題形式に対応し、実際と同じテスト形式で2回分の問題を掲載しています。TOEIC® Listening & Reading Test の受験準備にお使いください。

本シリーズの特長

- 問題は全て、ETSが実際のテストと同じプロセスで制作しています。
- サンプル問題とテスト2回分の問題（200問×2回、計400問）を掲載しています。
- 素点から参考スコア範囲が算出可能です。
- 正解を導くための詳しい解説と、学習の助けとなる語注を掲載しています。

音声について

- 本書で扱う音声は、専用のウェブサイトもしくはアプリでダウンロード・再生することができます。
- リスニングセクションの音声は全て、TOEIC®公式スピーカーによるものです。
- 特典として、TEST 1、2のリーディングセクションの以下の音声をご利用いただけます。問題に解答した後の学習用教材としてご活用ください。特典音声はリスニングセクションとは別に収録したもので、標準的な北米発音を採用しています。
  - 正解が入った問題音声（Part 5、6）
  - 文書の音声（Part 7）
- 音声を使った学習例については、別冊『解答・解説』p.6でご紹介していますのでご参照ください。

　本書が、TOEIC® Listening & Reading Testの出題形式の理解と受験準備、そして皆さまの英語学習のお役に立つことを願っております。

2024年7月
一般財団法人 国際ビジネスコミュニケーション協会

目　次

本冊

＊解答用紙はp.112の後ろに綴じ込まれています。

別冊 『解答・解説』

- 解答・解説で使われている表記の説明
- 音声ファイル　一覧表
- 音声を使った学習例の紹介
- 参考スコア範囲の算出方法
- 正解一覧
- 解答・解説

TOEIC® Listening & Reading Test について

TOEIC® Listening & Reading Test とは？

TOEIC® Listening & Reading Test（以下、TOEIC® L&R）は、TOEIC® Program のテストの一つで、英語における Listening（聞く）と Reading（読む）の力を測定します。結果は合格・不合格ではなく、リスニングセクション 5〜495 点、リーディングセクション 5〜495 点、トータル 10〜990 点のスコアで評価されます。スコアの基準は常に一定であり、 英語能力に変化がない限りスコアも一定に保たれます。知識・教養としての英語ではなく、オフィスや日常生活における英語によるコミュニケーション能力を幅広く測定するテストです。特定の文化を知らないと理解できない表現を排除しているので、誰もが公平に受けることができる「グローバルスタンダード」として活用されています。

問題形式

- リスニングセクション（約 45 分間・100 問）とリーディングセクション（75 分間・100 問）から成り、約 2 時間で 200 問に解答します。
- テストは英文のみで構成されており、英文和訳や和文英訳といった設問はありません。
- マークシート方式の一斉客観テストです。
- リスニングセクションにおける発音は、米国・英国・カナダ・オーストラリアが使われています。

  ＊テスト中、問題用紙への書き込みは一切禁じられています。

リスニングセクション（約 45 分間）

パート	Part Name	パート名	設問数
1	Photographs	写真描写問題	6
2	Question-Response	応答問題	25
3	Conversations	会話問題	39
4	Talks	説明文問題	30

リーディングセクション（75 分間）

パート	Part Name	パート名	設問数
5	Incomplete Sentences	短文穴埋め問題	30
6	Text Completion	長文穴埋め問題	16
7	• Single passages	1 つの文書	29
	• Multiple passages	複数の文書	25

開発・運営団体について

TOEIC® L&R は、ETS によって開発・制作されています。ETS は、米国ニュージャージー州プリンストンに拠点を置き、TOEIC® Program や TOEFL、GRE（大学院入学共通試験）を含む約 200 のテストプログラムを開発している世界最大の非営利テスト開発機関です。

日本における TOEIC® L&R を含む TOEIC® Program の実施・運営は、一般財団法人 国際ビジネスコミュニケーション協会（IIBC）が行っています。IIBC は、公式教材の出版やグローバル人材育成など、「人と企業の国際化」の推進に貢献するための活動を展開しています。

本書の構成と使い方

本書は、本冊と別冊に分かれています。それぞれの主な内容は以下の通りです。
- 本冊 …… 「サンプル問題」「TEST 1」「TEST 2」「解答用紙」
- 別冊『解答・解説』…… 「音声ファイル 一覧表」「音声を使った学習例の紹介」
「参考スコア範囲の算出方法」「正解一覧」「解答・解説」

本冊

サンプル問題（29問）［本冊p.8-27］

全パートから合計29問を掲載しています。 🔊 **002-010**

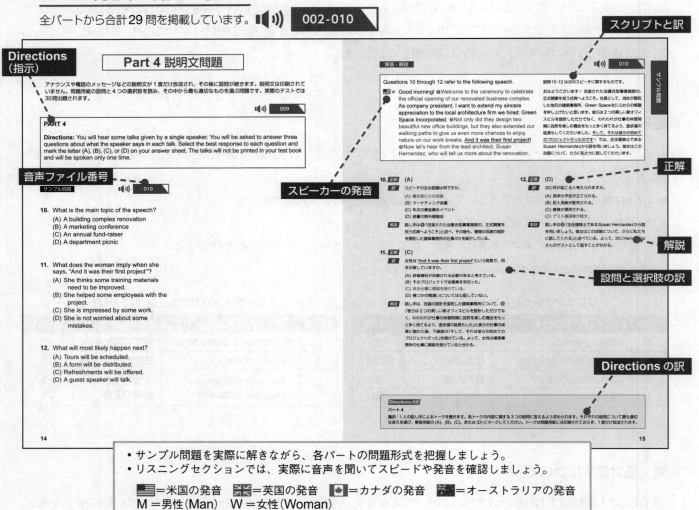

スクリプトと訳

Directions（指示）

Part 4 説明文問題

アナウンスや電話のメッセージなどの説明文が1度だけ放送され、その後に設問が続きます。説明文は印刷されていません。問題用紙の設問と4つの選択肢を読み、その中から最も適切なものを選ぶ問題です。実際のテストでは30問出題されます。

🔊 **009**

PART 4

Directions: You will hear some talks given by a single speaker. You will be asked to answer three questions about what the speaker says in each talk. Select the best response to each question and mark the letter (A), (B), (C), or (D) on your answer sheet. The talks will not be printed in your test book and will be spoken only one time.

音声ファイル番号

サンプル問題 🔊 **010**

10. What is the main topic of the speech?
(A) A building complex renovation
(B) A marketing conference
(C) An annual fund-raiser
(D) A department picnic

11. What does the woman imply when she says, "And it was their first project"?
(A) She thinks some training materials need to be improved.
(B) She helped some employees with the project.
(C) She is impressed by some work.
(D) She is not worried about some mistakes.

12. What will most likely happen next?
(A) Tours will be scheduled.
(B) A form will be distributed.
(C) Refreshments will be offered.
(D) A guest speaker will talk.

スピーカーの発音

解答・解説

Questions 10 through 12 refer to the following speech.

W Good morning! ❶Welcome to the ceremony to celebrate the official opening of our renovated business complex. As company president, I want to extend my sincere appreciation to the local architecture firm we hired: Green Space Incorporated. ❷Not only did they design two beautiful new office buildings, but they also extended our walking paths to give us even more chances to enjoy nature on our work breaks. And it was their first project! ❸Now let's hear from the lead architect, Susan Hernandez, who will tell us more about the renovation.

設問10-12は次のスピーチに関するものです。

おはようございます！改装された当複合型事業施設の、正式開業を祝う式典へようこそ。社長として、当社が委託した地元の建築事務所、Green Space社に心からの感謝を申し上げたいと思います。彼らは2つの美しい新オフィスビルを設計しただけでなく、われわれが仕事の休憩時間に自然を楽しむ機会をもっと多く持てるよう、遊歩道の延長もしてくださいました。そして、それは彼らの初めてのプロジェクトだったのです！では、主任建築士であるSusan Hernandezから話を伺いましょう。彼女はこの改装について、さらに私たちに話してくださいます。

10. **正解** (A)
訳 スピーチの主な話題は何ですか。
(A) 複合型ビルの改装
(B) マーケティング会議
(C) 年次の資金集めイベント
(D) 部署の野外親睦会

解説 話し手は❶改装された当複合型事業施設の、正式開業を祝う式典へようこそと述べ、その後も、建物の改装の設計を委託した建築事務所の仕事ぶりを紹介している。

11. **正解** (C)
訳 女性は "And it was their first project" という発言で、何を示唆していますか。
(A) 研修資料が改善される必要があると考えている。
(B) そのプロジェクトで従業員を手伝った。
(C) ある仕事に感銘を受けている。
(D) 幾つかの間違いについては心配していない。

解説 話し手は、改装の設計を委託した建築事務所について、❷「彼らは2つの美しい新オフィスビルを設計しただけでなく、われわれが仕事の休憩時間に自然を楽しむ機会をもっと多く持てるよう、遊歩道の延長もした」と彼らの仕事の成果に触れた後、下線部の「そして、それは彼らの初めてのプロジェクトだった」と続けている。よって、女性は建築事務所の仕事に感謝を受けていると分かる。

12. **正解** (D)
訳 次に何が起こると考えられますか。
(A) 見学の予定が立てられる。
(B) 記入用紙が配布される。
(C) 軽食が提供される。
(D) ゲスト講演者が話す。

解説 話し手は❸「主任建築士であるSusan Hernandezから話を伺いましょう。彼女はこの改装について、さらに私たちに話してくれる」と述べている。よって、次にHernandezさんがゲストとして話すことが分かる。

正解

解説

設問と選択肢の訳

Directions の訳

パート4

指示：1人の話し手によるトークを聞きます。各トークの内容に関する3つの設問に答えるよう求められます。それぞれの設問について最も適切な答えを選び、解答用紙の(A)、(B)、(C)、または(D)にマークしてください。トークは問題用紙には印刷されておらず、1度だけ放送されます。

14 / 15

- サンプル問題を実際に解きながら、各パートの問題形式を把握しましょう。
- リスニングセクションでは、実際に音声を聞いてスピードや発音を確認しましょう。

🇺🇸＝米国の発音　🇬🇧＝英国の発音　🇨🇦＝カナダの発音　🇦🇺＝オーストラリアの発音
M＝男性（Man）　W＝女性（Woman）

TEST 1 ［本冊p.29-70］ 🔊 **011-092**　　### TEST 2 ［本冊p.71-111］ 🔊 **150-231**

TEST 1、2ともに、実際のテストと同じ、合計200問で構成されています。

リスニングセクション	100問	約45分間
リーディングセクション	100問	75分間

予行演習として時間を計って解答し、時間配分の参考にしたり、伸ばしたい分野や弱点を把握したり、使い方を工夫してみましょう。

別冊『解答・解説』

音声ファイル 一覧表
[別冊 p.4-5]

参考スコア範囲の算出方法 [別冊 p.7]

正解数を基に、参考スコア範囲を算出できます。

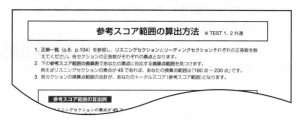

正解一覧 [TEST 1 → 別冊 p.8　TEST 2 → 別冊 p.104]

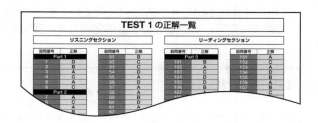

解答・解説 [TEST 1 → 別冊 p.9-103　TEST 2 → 別冊 p.105-199]

表記の説明は、別冊 p.2-3 をご覧ください。

問題の再掲載

問題の訳

語注
(Part 3、4、6、7)

設問と選択肢の訳

正解と解説

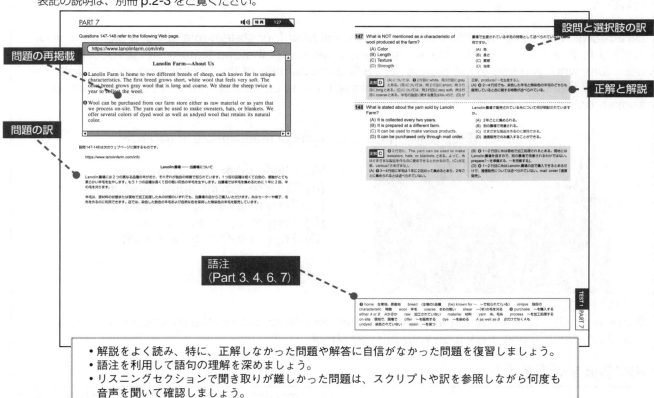

- 解説をよく読み、特に、正解しなかった問題や解答に自信がなかった問題を復習しましょう。
- 語注を利用して語句の理解を深めましょう。
- リスニングセクションで聞き取りが難しかった問題は、スクリプトや訳を参照しながら何度も音声を聞いて確認しましょう。

サンプル問題

TOEIC® Listening & Reading Test（以下、TOEIC® L&R）の問題形式を、サンプル問題を使ってご紹介します。サンプル問題は、全部で29問（リスニングセクション12問、リーディングセクション17問）です。サンプル問題の番号は、実際のテストの設問番号とは異なります。

TOEIC® L&Rのリスニングセクションは4つ、リーディングセクションは3つのパートに分かれています。問題用紙には、各パートの最初にDirectionsが英文で印刷されています。

Part 1 写真描写問題

1枚の写真について4つの短い説明文が1度だけ放送されます。説明文は印刷されていません。4つのうち写真を最も適切に描写しているものを選ぶ問題です。実際のテストでは6問出題されます。

🔊 002 ◢

LISTENING TEST

In the Listening test, you will be asked to demonstrate how well you understand spoken English. The entire Listening test will last approximately 45 minutes. There are four parts, and directions are given for each part. You must mark your answers on the separate answer sheet. Do not write your answers in your test book.

PART 1

Directions: For each question in this part, you will hear four statements about a picture in your test book. When you hear the statements, you must select the one statement that best describes what you see in the picture. Then find the number of the question on your answer sheet and mark your answer. The statements will not be printed in your test book and will be spoken only one time.

Look at the example item below.

Now listen to the four statements.
(A) They're moving some furniture.
(B) They're entering a meeting room.
(C) They're sitting at a table.
(D) They're cleaning the carpet.

Statement (C), "They're sitting at a table," is the best description of the picture, so you should select answer (C) and mark it on your answer sheet.

Now Part 1 will begin.

＊上記枠内の網掛けの部分は音声のみで、問題用紙には印刷されていません。

1.

解答・解説

1. Look at the picture marked number 1 in your test book.

🇦🇺 M　(A) A truck is stopped at a stoplight.
　　　(B) A man is using a gardening tool.
　　　(C) Some people are sitting on the grass.
　　　(D) Some workers are cutting down a tree.

正解　**(B)**

解説　gardeningは「造園、園芸」、toolは「用具、道具」という意味。

訳　問題用紙にある問題1の写真を見てください。

　　　(A) トラックが停止信号で止まっている。
　　　(B) 男性が造園用具を使っている。
　　　(C) 何人かの人々が芝生の上に座っている。
　　　(D) 何人かの作業員が木を切り倒している。

---

*Directions*の訳

リスニングテスト

リスニングテストでは、話されている英語をどのくらいよく理解しているかが問われます。リスニングテストは全体で約45分間です。4つのパートがあり、各パートにおいて指示が与えられます。答えは、別紙の解答用紙にマークしてください。問題用紙に答えを書き込んではいけません。

パート1

指示：このパートの各設問では、問題用紙にある写真について、4つの説明文を聞きます。説明文を聞いて、写真の内容を最も適切に描写しているものを選んでください。そして解答用紙の該当する設問番号にあなたの答えをマークしてください。説明文は問題用紙には印刷されておらず、1度だけ放送されます。

下の例題を見てください。

では4つの説明文を聞きましょう。
　(A) 彼らは家具を動かしている。
　(B) 彼らは会議室に入ろうとしている。
　(C) 彼らはテーブルのところに座っている。
　(D) 彼らはカーペットを掃除している。

(C)の文、"They're sitting at a table"(彼らはテーブルのところに座っている)がこの写真を最も適切に描写しているので、(C)を選び、解答用紙にマークします。

ではパート1が始まります。

Part 2 応答問題

1つの質問または発言と、3つの応答がそれぞれ1度だけ放送されます。質問も応答も印刷されていません。質問に対して最も適切な応答を選ぶ問題です。実際のテストでは25問出題されます。

 004

PART 2

Directions: You will hear a question or statement and three responses spoken in English. They will not be printed in your test book and will be spoken only one time. Select the best response to the question or statement and mark the letter (A), (B), or (C) on your answer sheet.

Now let us begin with question number 2.

＊上記枠内の網掛けの部分は音声のみで、問題用紙には印刷されていません。

サンプル問題

 005

2. Mark your answer on your answer sheet.
3. Mark your answer on your answer sheet.

解答・解説

2. 🇺🇸 W　Are you taking an international or a domestic flight?

　　🇦🇺 M　(A) I'd prefer a window seat.
　　　　　(B) He moved there last year.
　　　　　(C) I'm flying internationally.

正解 **(C)**

解説 *A or B*?の形で、国際線と国内線のどちらの便に乗るのかを尋ねているのに対し、「国際線の飛行機で行く」と答えている(C)が正解。

訳 あなたは国際線の便に乗りますか、それとも国内線の便ですか。

　　(A) 私は窓側の席を希望します。
　　(B) 彼は昨年、そこへ引っ越しました。
　　(C) 私は国際線の飛行機で行きます。

3. 🇨🇦 M　Shouldn't we hire more salespeople?

　　🇬🇧 W　(A) I'm glad they went.
　　　　　(B) A higher profit.
　　　　　(C) Let's look at the budget.

正解 **(C)**

解説 「もっと販売員を雇った方がいいのではないか」という男性の発言に対し、「予算を見てみよう」と雇用の検討を示唆している(C)が正解。

訳 私たちはもっと販売員を雇った方がいいのではありませんか。

　　(A) 私は、彼らが行ってうれしいです。
　　(B) より高い利益です。
　　(C) 予算を見てみましょう。

---

*Directions*の訳

パート2

指示: 英語による1つの質問または発言と、3つの応答を聞きます。それらは問題用紙には印刷されておらず、1度だけ放送されます。質問または発言に対して最も適切な応答を選び、解答用紙の(A)、(B)、または(C)にマークしてください。

では、設問2から始めましょう。

問題の訳

答えを解答用紙にマークしてください。

Part 3 会話問題

会話が1度だけ放送され、その後に設問が続きます。会話は印刷されていません。問題用紙の設問と4つの選択肢を読み、その中から最も適切なものを選ぶ問題です。実際のテストでは39問出題されます。

 006

PART 3

Directions: You will hear some conversations between two or more people. You will be asked to answer three questions about what the speakers say in each conversation. Select the best response to each question and mark the letter (A), (B), (C), or (D) on your answer sheet. The conversations will not be printed in your test book and will be spoken only one time.

  007

4. Which department is the man most likely calling?

(A) Receiving
(B) Catering
(C) Security
(D) Finance

5. Why does the man apologize?

(A) He has forgotten his badge.
(B) His report will be late.
(C) A meeting location has to be changed.
(D) A shipment must be delivered after business hours.

6. What does the woman say she will do?

(A) Arrange additional workspace
(B) Publish some materials
(C) Issue a temporary pass
(D) Ask staff to work late

 008

5th Annual Agricultural Fair

Day 1–Vegetables
Day 2–Dairy
Day 3–Flowers
Day 4–Baked goods

7. Why do the speakers want to attend the fair?

(A) To advertise a new business
(B) To find local food suppliers
(C) To sell some products
(D) To participate in a workshop

8. What does the man say he has downloaded?

(A) An electronic book
(B) A mobile phone application
(C) Some photographs
(D) Some tickets

9. Look at the graphic. Which day do the speakers decide to attend the fair?

(A) Day 1
(B) Day 2
(C) Day 3
(D) Day 4

11

Questions 4 through 6 refer to the following conversation. 　設問4-6 は次の会話に関するものです。

🇦🇺 M　Hello. ❶I'm expecting an extra-large load of clothing racks delivered to the store today, and they'll arrive after business hours. Are you the person I should inform about this?

もしもし。今日お店に、洋服ラックの特大の積み荷が配達される予定ですが、それらは営業時間の後に着きます。あなたがこの件についてお知らせすべき方でしょうか。

🇬🇧 W　Yes, ❷I'm head of Receiving. But ❸you're supposed to have suppliers make deliveries during business hours.

はい、私が荷受け部門の責任者です。でも、供給業者には、営業時間中に配達してもらうことになっているはずですが。

🇦🇺 M　❹I'm sorry, but this is the only time the supplier can deliver them, and we need the racks for a fashion show we're having tomorrow.

申し訳ありません。しかし、これが、供給業者がそれらを配達できる唯一の時間帯で、私たちが明日開催するファッションショーには、そのラックが必要なんです。

🇬🇧 W　I understand. ❺I'm not sure which of my staff members is working tonight, but I'll ask one of them to stay late to accept the delivery.

分かりました。今夜うちのスタッフの誰が勤務するのか定かではありませんが、配達物を受け取るために遅くまで残るよう、彼らのうちの1人に頼みます。

---

4. 正解　**(A)**

訳　男性はどの部署に電話をかけていると考えられますか。

(A) 荷受け
(B) ケータリング
(C) 警備
(D) 財務

解説　男性からの電話に応答した女性は ❷「私が荷受け部門の責任者だ」と答え、その後も2人は配達物の受け取りについて話をしている。

5. 正解　**(D)**

訳　男性はなぜ謝罪していますか。

(A) 自分のバッジを忘れたから。
(B) 報告書が遅れるから。
(C) 会議の場所が変更されなければならないから。
(D) 荷物が営業時間の後に配達されざるを得ないから。

解説　❶「積み荷が配達される予定だが、それらは営業時間の後に着く」という男性の報告に対し、女性が ❸「供給業者には、営業時間中に配達してもらうことになっているはず」と指摘している。それに対して男性は ❹で、「申し訳ない」と謝罪後「これが、供給業者がそれらを配達できる唯一の時間帯で、私たちが明日開催するファッションショーには、そのラックが必要だ」と事情を説明している。よって、正解は(D)。

6. 正解　**(D)**

訳　女性は何をすると言っていますか。

(A) 追加の作業スペースを手配する。
(B) 資料を公表する。
(C) 臨時の通行証を発行する。
(D) スタッフに遅くまで勤務するよう頼む。

解説　女性は ❺「今夜うちのスタッフの誰が勤務するのか定かではないが、配達物を受け取るために遅くまで残るよう、彼らのうちの1人に頼む」と述べている。stay late を work late「遅くまで勤務する」と表した(D)が正解。

Directionsの訳

パート3

指示：2人あるいはそれ以上の人々の会話を聞きます。各会話の内容に関する3つの設問に答えるよう求められます。それぞれの設問について最も適切な答えを選び、解答用紙の (A)、(B)、(C)、または (D) にマークしてください。会話は問題用紙には印刷されておらず、1度だけ放送されます。

Questions 7 through 9 refer to the following conversation and schedule.

🇺🇸 W　Pedro, ❶I know we're still looking for local fresh food suppliers for our new restaurant. We should check out the Agricultural Fair next month.

🇨🇦 M　That's a good idea. It's a major event, so many local farmers will be there. ❷I downloaded the fair's mobile phone application. The app has a lot of helpful information, including a schedule. Which day do you think we should go?

🇺🇸 W　Well, it looks like they'll have dairy vendors on the second day.

🇨🇦 M　Hmm, I just contacted a dairy company that might work for us. ❸We really need a vegetable supplier though…

🇺🇸 W　Oh, OK. ❹They have a day for showcasing vegetable farmers. Let's go then.

設問7-9 は次の会話と予定表に関するものです。

Pedro、私たちはまだ、うちの新しいレストランのために、地元の生鮮食品の供給業者を探しているわよね。来月の農業フェアを見てみるべきだわ。

それは良い考えだね。大きなイベントだから、多数の地元の農業経営者たちがそこにいるだろう。僕はフェアの携帯電話用アプリをダウンロードしたよ。このアプリには、予定表を含め、役立つ情報がたくさんあるんだ。僕たちはどの日に行くべきだと思う？

そうね、乳製品の販売業者は2日目にいるみたいね。

うーん、僕はうちに合いそうな乳製品会社に連絡を取ったばかりなんだ。僕たちには野菜の供給業者はぜひとも必要だけど…。

ああ、分かったわ。野菜農家の出展日があるわ。そのときに行きましょう。

---

7. 正解　**(B)**

訳　なぜ話し手たちはフェアに行きたいと思っていますか。

(A) 新しい店を宣伝するため。
(B) 地元の食品供給業者を見つけるため。
(C) 製品を販売するため。
(D) 講習会に参加するため。

解説　女性は❶「私たちはまだ、うちの新しいレストランのために、地元の生鮮食品の供給業者を探している。来月の農業フェアを見てみるべきだ」と提案し、男性もそれに同意している。よって、(B)が適切。

8. 正解　**(B)**

訳　男性は何をダウンロードしたと言っていますか。

(A) 電子書籍
(B) 携帯電話用アプリ
(C) 数枚の写真
(D) 数枚のチケット

解説　男性は❷「僕はフェアの携帯電話用アプリをダウンロードした」と述べている。

9. 正解　**(A)**

訳　図を見てください。話し手たちはどの日にフェアへ行くことに決めますか。

(A) 1日目
(B) 2日目
(C) 3日目
(D) 4日目

解説　❸「僕たちには野菜の供給業者がぜひとも必要だ」という男性の発言に対し、女性は❹「野菜農家の出展日がある。そのときに行こう」と提案している。予定表から、野菜農家が集まる日は1日目だと分かる。予定表のbaked goodsはクッキーやパンなどのオーブンで焼いた食品を指す。

図の訳

第5回　年次農業フェア
1日目 ― 野菜
2日目 ― 乳製品
3日目 ― 花
4日目 ― パン・焼き菓子

Part 4 説明文問題

アナウンスや電話のメッセージなどの説明文が1度だけ放送され、その後に設問が続きます。説明文は印刷されていません。問題用紙の設問と4つの選択肢を読み、その中から最も適切なものを選ぶ問題です。実際のテストでは30問出題されます。

 009

PART 4

Directions: You will hear some talks given by a single speaker. You will be asked to answer three questions about what the speaker says in each talk. Select the best response to each question and mark the letter (A), (B), (C), or (D) on your answer sheet. The talks will not be printed in your test book and will be spoken only one time.

サンプル問題 　　 010

10. What is the main topic of the speech?

(A) A building complex renovation
(B) A marketing conference
(C) An annual fund-raiser
(D) A department picnic

11. What does the woman imply when she says, "And it was their first project"?

(A) She thinks some training materials need to be improved.
(B) She helped some employees with the project.
(C) She is impressed by some work.
(D) She is not worried about some mistakes.

12. What will most likely happen next?

(A) Tours will be scheduled.
(B) A form will be distributed.
(C) Refreshments will be offered.
(D) A guest speaker will talk.

Questions 10 through 12 refer to the following speech.

🇺🇸 w Good morning! ❶Welcome to the ceremony to celebrate the official opening of our renovated business complex. As company president, I want to extend my sincere appreciation to the local architecture firm we hired: Green Space Incorporated. ❷Not only did they design two beautiful new office buildings, but they also extended our walking paths to give us even more chances to enjoy nature on our work breaks. <u>And it was their first project!</u> ❸Now let's hear from the lead architect, Susan Hernandez, who will tell us more about the renovation.

設問10-12 は次のスピーチに関するものです。

おはようございます！ 改装された当複合型事業施設の、正式開業を祝う式典へようこそ。社長として、当社が委託した地元の建築事務所、Green Space社に心からの感謝を申し上げたいと思います。彼らは2つの美しい新オフィスビルを設計しただけでなく、われわれが仕事の休憩時間に自然を楽しむ機会をもっと多く持てるよう、遊歩道の延長もしてくださいました。<u>そして、それは彼らの初めてのプロジェクトだったのです！</u> では、主任建築士であるSusan Hernandezから話を伺いましょう。彼女はこの改装について、さらに私たちに話してくださいます。

10. 正解 **(A)**

訳　スピーチの主な話題は何ですか。

(A) 複合型ビルの改装
(B) マーケティング会議
(C) 年次の資金集めイベント
(D) 部署の野外親睦会

解説　話し手は❶「改装された当複合型事業施設の、正式開業を祝う式典へようこそ」と述べ、その後も、建物の改装の設計を委託した建築事務所の仕事ぶりを紹介している。

11. 正解 **(C)**

訳　女性は"And it was their first project"という発言で、何を示唆していますか。

(A) 研修資料が改善される必要があると考えている。
(B) そのプロジェクトで従業員を手伝った。
(C) ある仕事に感銘を受けている。
(D) 幾つかの間違いについては心配していない。

解説　話し手は、改装の設計を委託した建築事務所について、❷「彼らは2つの美しい新オフィスビルを設計しただけでなく、われわれが仕事の休憩時間に自然を楽しむ機会をもっと多く持てるよう、遊歩道の延長もした」と彼らの仕事の成果に触れた後、下線部の「そして、それは彼らの初めてのプロジェクトだった」を続けている。よって、女性は建築事務所の仕事に感銘を受けていると分かる。

12. 正解 **(D)**

訳　次に何が起こると考えられますか。

(A) 見学の予定が立てられる。
(B) 記入用紙が配布される。
(C) 軽食が提供される。
(D) ゲスト講演者が話す。

解説　話し手は❸「主任建築士であるSusan Hernandezから話を伺いましょう。彼女はこの改装について、さらに私たちに話してくれる」と述べている。よって、次にHernandezさんがゲストとして話すことが分かる。

Directionsの訳

パート4

指示：1人の話し手によるトークを聞きます。各トークの内容に関する3つの設問に答えるよう求められます。それぞれの設問について最も適切な答えを選び、解答用紙の (A)、(B)、(C)、または (D) にマークしてください。トークは問題用紙には印刷されておらず、1度だけ放送されます。

Part 5 短文穴埋め問題

4つの選択肢の中から最も適切なものを選び、不完全な文を完成させる問題です。実際のテストでは30問出題されます。

READING TEST

In the Reading test, you will read a variety of texts and answer several different types of reading comprehension questions. The entire Reading test will last 75 minutes. There are three parts, and directions are given for each part. You are encouraged to answer as many questions as possible within the time allowed.

You must mark your answers on the separate answer sheet. Do not write your answers in your test book.

PART 5

Directions: A word or phrase is missing in each of the sentences below. Four answer choices are given below each sentence. Select the best answer to complete the sentence. Then mark the letter (A), (B), (C), or (D) on your answer sheet.

サンプル問題

13. Before ------- with the recruiter, applicants should sign in at the personnel department's reception desk.
    (A) meets
    (B) meeting
    (C) to meet
    (D) was met

14. Stefano Linen Company suggests requesting a small fabric ------- before placing your final order.
    (A) bonus
    (B) sample
    (C) feature
    (D) model

16

13. **正解** **(B)**

訳 採用担当者と会う前に、応募者の方々は人事部の受付で署名して到着を記録してください。

(A) 動詞の三人称単数現在形
(B) 動名詞
(C) to不定詞
(D) 受動態の過去形

解説 選択肢は全て動詞meet「会う」の変化した形。文頭からカンマまでの部分に主語と動詞がないため、Beforeは前置詞と考えられる。前置詞に続く空所には名詞の働きをする語句が入るので、動名詞の(B) meetingが適切である。sign in「署名して到着を記録する」。

14. **正解** **(B)**

訳 Stefanoリネン社は、お客さまが最終的な注文をなさる前に、小さな布地見本をご要望になることをお勧めしています。

(A) 特別手当
(B) 見本
(C) 特徴
(D) 模型

解説 選択肢は全て名詞。空所の後ろは「お客さまが最終的な注文をする前に」という意味。(B) sample「見本」を空所に入れるとsmall fabric sample「小さな布地見本」となり、注文前に要望するものとして適切で、意味が通る。

Directionsの訳

リーディングテスト

リーディングテストでは、さまざまな文章を読んで、読解力を測る何種類かの問題に答えます。リーディングテストは全体で75分間です。3つのパートがあり、各パートにおいて指示が与えられます。制限時間内に、できるだけ多くの設問に答えてください。

答えは、別紙の解答用紙にマークしてください。問題用紙に答えを書き込んではいけません。

パート5

指示：以下の各文において語や句が抜けています。各文の下には選択肢が4つ与えられています。文を完成させるのに最も適切な答えを選びます。そして解答用紙の (A)、(B)、(C)、または (D) にマークしてください。

Part 6 長文穴埋め問題

4つの選択肢の中から最も適切なものを選び、不完全な文書を完成させる問題です。実際のテストでは16問出題されます。

PART 6

Directions: Read the texts that follow. A word, phrase, or sentence is missing in parts of each text. Four answer choices for each question are given below the text. Select the best answer to complete the text. Then mark the letter (A), (B), (C), or (D) on your answer sheet.

サンプル問題

Questions 15-18 refer to the following article.

❶ SAN DIEGO (May 5)—Matino Industries has just bolstered its image with environmentally conscious customers thanks to its ------- to reduce its use of nonrenewable energy to less
than 20 percent within five years. -------. Best practices guidelines are already being revised
------- powering down and disconnecting equipment when not in use. In addition, solar-panel
arrays are slated for installation on-site as early as next year. When weather ------- are clear,
these panels will offset Matino's reliance on the power grid, as they already do for a growing
list of companies.

15. **16.** **17.** **18.**

*❶は解説の中で説明している文書中の段落番号等を示しています。問題用紙には印刷されていません。

---

15. (A) product
(B) commitment
(C) contest
(D) workforce

16. (A) Discounts on all its products have
increased Matino's customer base.
(B) Management predicts that the takeover
will result in a net financial gain.
(C) To achieve this goal, the company will
begin by improving its energy efficiency.
(D) The initial step will involve redesigning
the company's logo and slogans.

17. (A) been encouraging
(B) have encouraged
(C) encourages
(D) to encourage

18. (A) conditions
(B) instructions
(C) views
(D) reports

設問15-18は次の記事に関するものです。

サンディエゴ（5月5日）──Matino産業社は、同社の再生不能エネルギーの使用を5年以内に20パーセント未満に削減するという公約のおかげで、環境意識の高い顧客にとっての同社のイメージを強化したところである。*この目標を達成するために同社は、自社のエネルギー効率を改善することから始める予定だ。機器を使用していないときには電源を落として接続を切ることを推奨するために、最良実践ガイドラインがすでに改定されているところである。さらに、早くも来年には、ソーラーパネルの列が構内に設置される予定である。天候条件が晴れのときには、これらのパネルが、増え続ける多くの企業に対してすでにそうしているように、Matino社の送電網依存を弱めることになる。

*設問16の挿入文の訳

15. 正解 **(B)**

訳 (A) 製品
(B) 公約
(C) 競争
(D) 全従業員

解説 ❶の1～3行目は「Matino産業社は、同社の-------のおかげで、同社のイメージを強化したところだ」というのが、文の中心の意味。空所の後ろの「同社の再生不能エネルギーの使用を5年以内に20パーセント未満に削減すること」は、空所に入る名詞の内容を示していると考えられるので、文意から(B) commitment「公約」が適切。

16. 正解 **(C)**

訳 (A) 全ての自社製品に対する割引が、Matino社の顧客基盤を拡大してきた。
(B) 経営陣は、その企業買収は財務上の純利益をもたらすと予測している。
(C) この目標を達成するために同社は、自社のエネルギー効率を改善することから始める予定だ。
(D) 第1段階には、会社のロゴとスローガンを作り直すことが含まれる予定だ。

解説 空所の前の文では、Matino産業社が同社の再生不能エネルギーの使用を5年以内に20パーセント未満に削減することが述べられている。この内容をthis goalで受けて、目標達成のために同社がこれから取り組むことを挙げている(C)が流れとして適切。

17. 正解 **(D)**

訳 (A) 〈be動詞の過去分詞＋現在分詞〉
(B) 現在完了形
(C) 動詞の三人称単数現在形
(D) to不定詞

解説 選択肢は全て動詞encourage「～を推奨する」が変化した形。空所の前に〈主語＋動詞〉の形があり、andやorなどの接続詞もないことから、空所に動詞は入らない。空所には、to不定詞の(D) to encourageが適切。

18. 正解 **(A)**

訳 (A) 条件
(B) 指示
(C) 見解
(D) 報道

解説 空所を含む文の、文頭からカンマまでは「天候-------が晴れのときには」という意味。these panels以降では、その際にソーラーパネルがもたらす効果について述べられている。「天候条件が晴れのときには」とすると意味が通るため、(A) conditions「条件」が適切。

***Directions*の訳**

パート6

指示：以下の文書を読んでください。各文書の中で語や句、または文が部分的に抜けています。文書の下には各設問の選択肢が4つ与えられています。文書を完成させるのに最も適切な答えを選びます。そして解答用紙の(A)、(B)、(C)、または(D)にマークしてください。

Part 7 読解問題

いろいろな形式の、1つもしくは複数の文書に関する問題が出題されます。設問と4つの選択肢を読み、その中から最も適切なものを選ぶ問題です。実際のテストでは1つの文書に関する設問が29問、複数の文書に関する設問が25問出題されます。

PART 7

Directions: In this part you will read a selection of texts, such as magazine and newspaper articles, e-mails, and instant messages. Each text or set of texts is followed by several questions. Select the best answer for each question and mark the letter (A), (B), (C), or (D) on your answer sheet.

サンプル問題

Questions 19-20 refer to the following text-message chain.

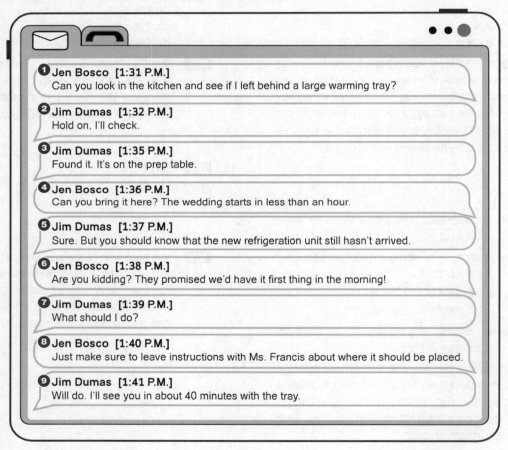

① Jen Bosco [1:31 P.M.]
Can you look in the kitchen and see if I left behind a large warming tray?

② Jim Dumas [1:32 P.M.]
Hold on, I'll check.

③ Jim Dumas [1:35 P.M.]
Found it. It's on the prep table.

④ Jen Bosco [1:36 P.M.]
Can you bring it here? The wedding starts in less than an hour.

⑤ Jim Dumas [1:37 P.M.]
Sure. But you should know that the new refrigeration unit still hasn't arrived.

⑥ Jen Bosco [1:38 P.M.]
Are you kidding? They promised we'd have it first thing in the morning!

⑦ Jim Dumas [1:39 P.M.]
What should I do?

⑧ Jen Bosco [1:40 P.M.]
Just make sure to leave instructions with Ms. Francis about where it should be placed.

⑨ Jim Dumas [1:41 P.M.]
Will do. I'll see you in about 40 minutes with the tray.

---

19. For whom do the writers most likely work?

(A) A catering company
(B) A home-improvement store
(C) A kitchen-design company
(D) An appliance manufacturer

20. At 1:38 P.M., what does Ms. Bosco most likely mean when she writes, "Are you kidding"?

(A) She thinks Mr. Dumas is exaggerating.
(B) She knew she would have to wait a long time.
(C) She expects the refrigeration unit to arrive soon.
(D) She is upset that a delivery has not been made.

設問19-20は次のテキストメッセージのやり取りに関するものです。

> Jen Bosco [午後 1 時 31 分]
> 調理場の中をのぞいて、私が大きな保温トレーを置き忘れたかどうかを確かめてくれるかしら。
>
> Jim Dumas [午後 1 時 32 分]
> 待ってて、確認するよ。
>
> Jim Dumas [午後 1 時 35 分]
> 見つけた。調理台の上にあるよ。
>
> Jen Bosco [午後 1 時 36 分]
> それをここに持ってきてくれる？ 結婚式が 1 時間足らずで始まるの。
>
> Jim Dumas [午後 1 時 37 分]
> もちろん。でも、新しい冷蔵装置がまだ届いていないことを知っておいた方がいいよ。
>
> Jen Bosco [午後 1 時 38 分]
> 冗談でしょう？ 朝一番には私たちにそれを届けてくれると、彼らは約束したのよ。
>
> Jim Dumas [午後 1 時 39 分]
> 僕はどうしたらいい？
>
> Jen Bosco [午後 1 時 40 分]
> とにかく、どこにそれを置けばいいか、Francis さんに必ず指示を残しておいて。
>
> Jim Dumas [午後 1 時 41 分]
> そうするよ。約 40 分後にトレーを持って君に会うね。

19. 正解 **(A)**

訳 書き手たちはどこに勤めていると考えられますか。

(A) ケータリング会社
(B) ホームセンター
(C) キッチン設計会社
(D) 電化製品メーカー

解説 ❶と❷のやり取りから、書き手たちの職場には調理場があることが分かる。また❹で、BoscoさんがDumasさんに保温トレーを結婚式の場に持ってくるよう伝えていることから、書き手たちは料理を作り配達を行っていると考えられる。よって、(A)が適切。

20. 正解 **(D)**

訳 午後 1 時 38 分にBoscoさんは、"Are you kidding"という発言で、何を意味していると考えられますか。

(A) Dumasさんが誇張していると思っている。
(B) 長い間待たなくてはならないことを知っていた。
(C) 冷蔵装置がもうすぐ届くだろうと見込んでいる。
(D) 配達が行われていないことに動揺している。

解説 Dumasさんが❺「新しい冷蔵装置がまだ届いていないことを知っておいた方がいい」と伝えたのに対して、Boscoさんは「冗談でしょう？」と驚きを示し、「朝一番には私たちにそれを届けてくれると、彼らは約束した」と続けている。つまり、Boscoさんは配達が約束通りに行われていないことに動揺していると考えられる。

Directions の訳

パート 7

指示：このパートでは、雑誌や新聞の記事、Eメールやインスタントメッセージなどのさまざまな文書を読みます。1 つの文書または複数の文書のセットにはそれぞれ、幾つかの設問が続いています。各設問について最も適切な答えを選び、解答用紙の (A)、(B)、(C)、または (D) にマークしてください。

Questions 21-24 refer to the following Web page.

---

http://straubuniversityschoolofmedicine.edu/vendors/rfp0023

❶Straub University School of Medicine is currently seeking a vendor to provide surgical gloves, laboratory coats, and protective goggles. The university requires high-quality, hospital-grade equipment for its students and faculty and is especially interested in providers who currently work with local hospitals and clinics.

❷You can download the complete Request for Proposal (RFP) instructions from our Web site. Below is a summary of the proposal requirements. — [1] —.

• A standard proposal form, which can be downloaded from our Web site
• A general description of the provider and its experience in the industry
• Product descriptions with a complete list of specifications and prices
• Contact information of three current or recent clients who are able to speak to the quality of the provider's products or services

❸If you have any questions about the RFP, please submit them in writing to queries@straub.edu by July 20. — [2] —. Responses to questions will be posted publicly on the Straub University School of Medicine's Web page on August 4.

❹Proposals must be received no later than August 15. — [3] —. All submissions will be thoroughly reviewed, and the winning proposal will be announced on September 10. A contract will be finalized with the strongest candidate that same month, and the agreement will take effect starting October 1. — [4] —.

---

21. Who are the instructions intended for?

(A) Sellers of medical supplies
(B) Applicants for hospital jobs
(C) Hospital administrators
(D) Medical students

22. What are candidates required to submit?

(A) Questions about the proposal
(B) Professional references
(C) An application fee
(D) Product samples

23. When will candidates learn if they have been selected?

(A) In July
(B) In August
(C) In September
(D) In October

24. In which of the positions marked [1], [2], [3], and [4] does the following sentence best belong?

"All documentation must arrive by this date in a sealed envelope addressed to the School of Medicine's Purchasing Department."

(A) [1]
(B) [2]
(C) [3]
(D) [4]

設問21-24は次のウェブページに関するものです。

http://straubuniversityschoolofmedicine.edu/vendors/rfp0023

Straub 大学医学部は現在、手術用手袋、白衣、保護用ゴーグルを供給してくれる業者を求めています。本学は、学生と教授陣向けの、高品質で病院仕様の備品を必要としており、特に、地元の病院や診療所と現在取引をしている販売会社に関心があります。

本学のウェブサイトから、提案依頼書（RFP）の指示一式をダウンロードすることができます。以下は提案要件の概略です。

・定型の提案書式。本学のウェブサイトからダウンロード可能
・販売会社の概要および業界における同社の経験
・仕様および価格の全一覧を付した、製品の説明
・販売会社の製品あるいはサービスの質について述べることのできる、現在もしくは最近の顧客 3 社の連絡先

RFP について何かご質問がございましたら、それらを文書で 7 月 20 日までに queries@straub.edu 宛てにご提出ください。ご質問に対する回答は、8 月 4 日に Straub 大学医学部のウェブページ上で公開されます。

提案書は 8 月 15 日必着です。*全ての書類は、封書でこの日付までに医学部の購買部宛てに到着しなければなりません。全ての提出物は入念に検討され、採用された提案書は 9 月 10 日に発表されます。契約書は最有力候補業者とその同月に最終的な形にされ、契約は 10 月 1 日より発効します。

*設問 24 の挿入文の訳

21. 正解 **(A)**

訳　この指示は誰に向けられていますか。

(A) 医療用品の販売会社
(B) 病院の職への応募者
(C) 病院の管理者
(D) 医学生

解説　❶1～2行目に「Straub 大学医学部は現在、手術用手袋、白衣、保護用ゴーグルを供給する業者を求めている」とあり、❷では提案要件の概略について、❹では提出期日や選考過程などについて説明されている。よって、この指示は医療用品の販売会社に向けたものだと分かる。

22. 正解 **(B)**

訳　候補者は何を提出することを求められていますか。

(A) 提案書に関する質問
(B) 取引上の照会先
(C) 申込金
(D) 製品の見本

解説　❷で提案要件の概略として挙げられている箇条書きの 4 点目に、「販売会社の製品あるいはサービスの質について述べることのできる、現在もしくは最近の顧客 3 社の連絡先」とある。

23. 正解 **(C)**

訳　候補者はいつ、自分が選出されたかどうかを知りますか。

(A) 7 月
(B) 8 月
(C) 9 月
(D) 10 月

解説　❹2行目に、the winning proposal will be announced on September 10「採用された提案書は 9 月 10 日に発表される」とある。

24. 正解 **(C)**

訳　[1]、[2]、[3]、[4]と記載された箇所のうち、次の文が入るのに最もふさわしいのはどれですか。

「全ての書類は、封書でこの日付までに医学部の購買部宛てに到着しなければなりません」

(A) [1]
(B) [2]
(C) [3]
(D) [4]

解説　挿入文は書類の提出方法と宛先を伝えている。(C) [3]に入れると、挿入文中の this date「この日付」が❹1行目の August 15 を指し、提案書の提出期日に続けて提出方法と宛先を伝える自然な流れとなる。

Questions 25-29 refer to the following article, e-mail, and Web page.

❶ (November 6)—The Rudi's store at 47 Kask Highway in Glencoe Park will shut its doors next Saturday, adding another empty building to the local landscape. The shutdown is one of a rash of store closings in the greater Billington area and is a result of two major forces. First, Rudi's has changed its business plan, relying increasingly on online sales. Second, much of the traffic on Kask Highway has been rerouted to the recently completed bypass, resulting in fewer potential customers passing through Billington.

❷ Other Rudi's closings over the past two years include the store at 38 Quail Hill Road, the store at 21 Lowell Boulevard, and the downtown megastore at 59 Claremont Street on the banks of the Corks River. A Rudi's spokesperson stated that no further closures are expected.

To:	nathanpaugh@ioscodesign.com
From:	ccovey@tedesintl.com
Subject:	Tedes Building
Date:	January 25

Dear Mr. Paugh,

❶ The preliminary drawings you sent are right on target. I think your proposal to demolish most of the east wall and install floor-to-ceiling windows is terrific. If we were to leave everything as it now is, we would end up with a rather somber interior.

❷ Let's keep the current stairway where it is so that people can walk straight through the entrance and up to the second floor meeting rooms. We can configure the remaining area in the center of the first floor as open work space, with the executive offices off to the left side against the west wall. Including a large picture window at the entrance to the fitness center in the back of the first floor space is also a good idea.

❸ Please move forward with drawing up draft plans for our board's approval.

Thank you,

Cynthia Covey

http://www.buildingmonthly.com/readersreviews

| HOME | LATEST ISSUE | **READERS' REVIEWS** | ADVERTISERS |

The new Tedes corporate building
Posted by Monty K.

❶ Tedes International has opened its corporate headquarters in a former Rudi's megastore building. In an area with many vacated retail buildings, one is now a workplace for over 400 Tedes employees. Corporations looking for prime real estate should take notice.

❷ The interior design of the Tedes Building is notable for its mixed use of open and closed space. The entrance is open and inviting and leads to a wide staircase up to the second floor, which houses offices for upper management. Large windows installed as one of the exterior walls create a bright atmosphere in the open work space and nearby meeting rooms, while boats glide by on the river right in front of them. On my visit, several employees were exercising on fitness bikes in full view at the rear of the first-floor space.

25. What is the purpose of the article?

(A) To notify readers of recent job openings
(B) To publicize an online sale
(C) To report on a store closing
(D) To alert motorists to changing traffic patterns

26. Who most likely is Mr. Paugh?

(A) An artist
(B) An architect
(C) A real estate agent
(D) A reporter

27. Which former Rudi's location did Tedes International choose for its headquarters?

(A) 47 Kask Highway
(B) 38 Quail Hill Road
(C) 21 Lowell Boulevard
(D) 59 Claremont Street

28. What aspect of the design suggested by Ms. Covey was ultimately rejected?

(A) The replacement of a wall with windows
(B) The layout of the entrance
(C) The inclusion of a fitness center
(D) The location of the offices

29. What is implied by the reviewer?

(A) Tedes International is planning to expand.
(B) Tedes International wants to sell its property.
(C) Vacant buildings have great potential.
(D) Local businesses may experience reduced profits.

設問25-29は次の記事、Eメール、ウェブページに関するものです。

1. 記事

（11月6日）——グレンコーパークのカスク街道47番地にあるRudi's社の店舗は、次の土曜日に扉を閉ざし、その地域の風景にもう1棟空きビルを加えることになる。この閉店は、ビリントン広域圏で頻発する店舗の閉鎖の1つであり、2つの大きな影響力によるものである。第1に、Rudi's社が事業計画を変更し、オンライン販売に一層依存するようになったこと。第2に、カスク街道の交通の大部分が、最近完成した迂回路の方へ流れ、ビリントンを通る潜在顧客が減少する結果となったことだ。

過去2年間のRudi's社の他の閉店には、クウェイルヒル通り38番地の店舗、ローウェル大通り21番地の店舗、そしてコークス川岸のクレアモント通り59番地にあった中心街の超大型店舗が含まれる。Rudi's社の広報担当者は、これ以上の閉店は一切予定されていないと明言した。

2. Eメール

受信者：nathanpaugh@ioscodesign.com
送信者：ccovey@tedesintl.com
件名：　Tedes ビル
日付：　1月25日

Paugh様

お送りくださった仮の図面は、まさに期待通りのものです。東側の壁の大半を取り壊し、床から天井までの窓を設置するという貴殿のご提案は素晴らしいと思います。もし何もかも現状のままにしておいたとしたら、最終的にかなり陰気な内装になってしまうでしょう。

今の階段は、そのままの場所で残しましょう。そうすれば人々が入り口をまっすぐ通り抜け、2階の会議室に歩いて上がっていけます。1階の中央にある残りの区域は開放的な作業スペースとし、重役の執務室を左側へ、西の壁際に配置することができます。1階スペースの奥にあるフィットネスセンターへの入り口に大きな一枚ガラスの窓を入れることも良いアイデアです。

当社役員会の承認に向けて、設計図の草案の作成を進めてください。

よろしくお願いいたします。

Cynthia Covey

3. ウェブページ

http://www.buildingmonthly.com/readersreviews

| ホーム | 最新号 | 読者レビュー | 広告主 |

Tedes 社の新しいビル
Monty K. 投稿

Tedesインターナショナル社は、かつてRudi's社の超大型店舗だった建物に本社を開設した。空き家となった小売店のビルが多数ある地域において、1棟は今や400名超のTedes社の従業員の職場である。優良な不動産を求めている企業は注目すべきである。

Tedes ビルの内部設計は、開放的スペースと閉鎖的スペースを取り混ぜて使用していることで注目に値する。入り口は広々として、いざなうようであり、2階に至る広い階段に通じている。2階には、経営上層部のための執務室が入っている。外壁の一部として設置された大型の窓は、開放的な作業スペースと近くの会議室に明るい雰囲気を作り出し、他方で、すぐ目の前にある川をボートが滑るように進む。私の訪問時には、数名の従業員が1階スペースの奥で、よく見える所でフィットネスバイクで運動をしていた。

25. 正解 **(C)**

訳 記事の目的は何ですか。

(A) 読者に最近の求人を知らせること。
(B) オンラインのセールを宣伝すること。
(C) 店舗の閉鎖を報道すること。
(D) 車を運転する人に、交通パターンの変化について注意を喚起すること。

解説 **1**の記事の**①**1～3行目に、「グレンコーパークのカスク街道47番地にあるRudi's社の店舗は、次の土曜日に扉を閉ざす」とあり、その後も閉店の要因などが述べられている。よって、記事の目的はRudi's社の店舗の閉鎖を報道することだと分かる。

26. 正解 **(B)**

訳 Paughさんとは誰だと考えられますか。

(A) 芸術家
(B) 建築家
(C) 不動産仲介人
(D) 記者

解説 Paughさんは**2**のEメールの受信者。Eメールの本文では、**①**1行目で「お送りくださった仮の図面は、まさに期待通りのものだ」と伝えられ、建物の設計についての話が続いている。さらに、**③**で「設計図の草案の作成を進めてほしい」と依頼を受けていることから、Paughさんは建築家と考えられる。

27. 正解 **(D)**

訳 Tedesインターナショナル社は、かつてのRudi's社のどの場所を本社に選びましたか。

(A) カスク街道47番地
(B) クウェイルヒル通り38番地
(C) ローウェル大通り21番地
(D) クレアモント通り59番地

解説 **3**のウェブページの**①**1～2行目に、「Tedesインターナショナル社は、かつてRudi's社の超大型店舗だった建物に本社を開設した」とある。**1**の記事の**②**3～5行目に、閉店したRudi's社の店舗の1つとして、「コークス川岸のクレアモント通り59番地にあった中心街の超大型店舗」が挙げられているので、(D)が正解。

28. 正解 **(D)**

訳 Coveyさんによって示された設計のどの点が、最終的に不採用とされましたか。

(A) 壁を窓で置き換えること
(B) 入り口の配置
(C) フィットネスセンターを含めること
(D) 執務室の位置

解説 Coveyさんは**2**のEメールの送信者。仮の図面を作ったPaughさんに対して、**②**2～4行目で「1階の中央にある残りの区域は開放的な作業スペースとし、重役の執務室を左側へ、西の壁際に配置することができる」と述べている。一方、完成したビルの読者レビューを載せた**3**のウェブページには、**②**2～3行目に「入り口は広々として、いざなうようであり、2階に至る広い階段に通じている。2階には、経営上層部のための執務室が入っている」とあることから、重役の執務室はCoveyさんが提案した1階ではなく、2階に配置されたと分かる。

29. 正解 **(C)**

訳 レビュー投稿者によって何が示唆されていますか。

(A) Tedesインターナショナル社は拡大する予定である。
(B) Tedesインターナショナル社は同社の不動産を売却したいと思っている。
(C) 空きビルは大きな可能性を持っている。
(D) 地元の企業は減益を経験するかもしれない。

解説 **3**のウェブページの読者レビューの**①**1～3行目で、Tedesインターナショナル社がかつてRudi's社の超大型店舗だった建物に本社を開設したことで、空きビル1棟が今や多数の従業員の職場へと変化したことが述べられている。続けて「優良な不動産を求めている企業は注目すべきだ」とあることから、レビュー投稿者は空きビルに大きな可能性があることを示唆していると考えられる。

採点・結果について

TOEIC® Listening & Reading Test のテスト結果は合格・不合格ではなく、リスニングセクション5〜495点、リーディングセクション5〜495点、トータル10〜990点のスコアで、5点刻みで表示されます。このスコアは、常に評価基準を一定に保つために統計処理が行われ、英語能力に変化がない限りスコアも一定に保たれる点が大きな特長です。

テスト結果は以下の方法でお知らせいたします。
※スケジュールは、日米の祝日の影響により、遅れる場合があります。

- **● 試験日から17日後：インターネットでスコア表示**
  表示開始後、ご登録Eメールアドレスへご案内のメールを送信いたしますので、TOEIC申込サイトからログインしてご覧ください。

- **● 試験日から19日後：デジタル公式認定証を発行**
  スコア表示日の2日後を目途に、同じページで確認できます。TOEIC申込サイトからログインしてご覧ください。

Your Score（スコア）:
今回取得したリスニング、リーディングの各セクションスコアです。右側にトータルスコアが記載されます。

Percentile Rank（パーセンタイルランク）:
あなたが取得したスコアに満たない受験者が全体でどのくらいを占めているかをパーセンテージで示しています。
例えば、リスニングでスコア300点、パーセンタイルランクが41%という場合には、リスニングスコア300点未満の受験者が全体の41%いることを示します。つまり、リスニングスコア300点を取得した受験者は上位59%に位置することになります。

Score Descriptors（スコアディスクリプターズ）:
レベル別評価です。今回取得したスコアをもとに、あなたの英語運用能力上の長所が書かれています。

Abilities Measured（アビリティーズメジャード）:
項目別正答率です。リスニング、リーディングの5つの項目における正答率を示しています。

デジタル公式認定証のサンプル

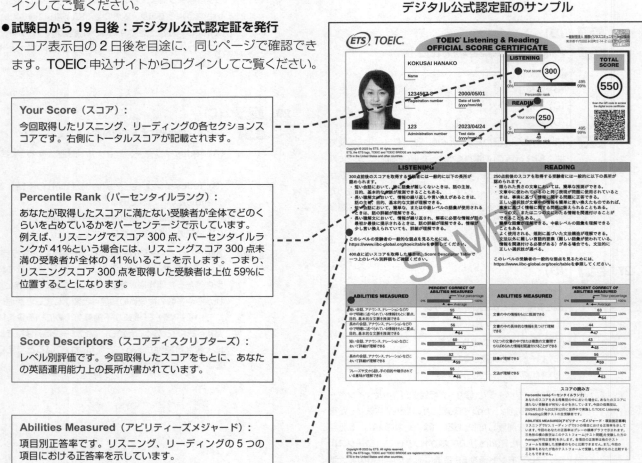

TOEIC® Listening & Reading 公開テストのお申し込み

IIBC公式サイト https://www.iibc-global.org にてテスト日程、申込方法、注意事項をご確認の上、申込受付期間内にお申し込みください。試験の実施方法などに変更があった場合にはIIBC公式サイト等でご案内いたします。

お問い合わせ

一般財団法人 国際ビジネスコミュニケーション協会　IIBC 試験運営センター
〒100-0014　東京都千代田区永田町 2-14-2　山王グランドビル
TEL：03-5521-6033（土・日・祝日・年末年始を除く 10:00 〜 17:00）

TEST 1

011-092

| LISTENING TEST | ···························· | **p.30** |
| READING TEST | ···························· | **p.42** |

＊解答用紙は本冊 p.112 の後ろに綴じ込まれています。

実際のテストでは問題用紙の裏側に、以下のようなテスト全体についての指示が印刷されています。この指示を念頭において、テストに取り組みましょう。

General Directions

This test is designed to measure your English language ability. The test is divided into two sections: Listening and Reading.

You must mark all of your answers on the separate answer sheet. For each question, you should select the best answer from the answer choices given. Then, on your answer sheet, you should find the number of the question and fill in the space that corresponds to the letter of the answer that you have selected. If you decide to change an answer, completely erase your old answer and then mark your new answer.

訳

全体についての指示

このテストはあなたの英語言語能力を測定するよう設計されています。テストはリスニングとリーディングという2つのセクションに分けられています。

答えは全て別紙の解答用紙にマークしてください。それぞれの設問について、与えられた選択肢から最も適切な答えを選びます。そして解答用紙の該当する設問番号に、選択した答えを塗りつぶしてください。答えを修正する場合は、元の答えを完全に消してから新しい答えをマークしてください。

LISTENING TEST

In the Listening test, you will be asked to demonstrate how well you understand spoken English. The entire Listening test will last approximately 45 minutes. There are four parts, and directions are given for each part. You must mark your answers on the separate answer sheet. Do not write your answers in your test book.

PART 1

Directions: For each question in this part, you will hear four statements about a picture in your test book. When you hear the statements, you must select the one statement that best describes what you see in the picture. Then find the number of the question on your answer sheet and mark your answer. The statements will not be printed in your test book and will be spoken only one time.

Statement (C), "They're sitting at a table," is the best description of the picture, so you should select answer (C) and mark it on your answer sheet.

1.

2.

GO ON TO THE NEXT PAGE ▶

3.

4.

5.

6.

GO ON TO THE NEXT PAGE ➡

PART 2

Directions: You will hear a question or statement and three responses spoken in English. They will not be printed in your test book and will be spoken only one time. Select the best response to the question or statement and mark the letter (A), (B), or (C) on your answer sheet.

7. Mark your answer on your answer sheet.

8. Mark your answer on your answer sheet.

9. Mark your answer on your answer sheet.

10. Mark your answer on your answer sheet.

11. Mark your answer on your answer sheet.

12. Mark your answer on your answer sheet.

13. Mark your answer on your answer sheet.

14. Mark your answer on your answer sheet.

15. Mark your answer on your answer sheet.

16. Mark your answer on your answer sheet.

17. Mark your answer on your answer sheet.

18. Mark your answer on your answer sheet.

19. Mark your answer on your answer sheet.

20. Mark your answer on your answer sheet.

21. Mark your answer on your answer sheet.

22. Mark your answer on your answer sheet.

23. Mark your answer on your answer sheet.

24. Mark your answer on your answer sheet.

25. Mark your answer on your answer sheet.

26. Mark your answer on your answer sheet.

27. Mark your answer on your answer sheet.

28. Mark your answer on your answer sheet.

29. Mark your answer on your answer sheet.

30. Mark your answer on your answer sheet.

31. Mark your answer on your answer sheet.

PART 3

Directions: You will hear some conversations between two or more people. You will be asked to answer three questions about what the speakers say in each conversation. Select the best response to each question and mark the letter (A), (B), (C), or (D) on your answer sheet. The conversations will not be printed in your test book and will be spoken only one time.

32. Where does the conversation most likely take place?
    (A) At a grocery store
    (B) At a kitchen supply store
    (C) At a restaurant
    (D) At a cooking school

33. What has caused a delay?
    (A) Bad weather
    (B) Roadwork
    (C) An order error
    (D) A staff shortage

34. Why does the man apologize?
    (A) An item is unavailable.
    (B) A price has changed.
    (C) A machine is not working.
    (D) An explanation is incorrect.

35. What are the speakers preparing?
    (A) A newsletter
    (B) A sales report
    (C) A presentation
    (D) A production schedule

36. What problem does the woman mention?
    (A) Some pages are missing.
    (B) A draft is late.
    (C) A detail is inaccurate.
    (D) The quality of a print job is poor.

37. What does the man say he will do tomorrow?
    (A) Send an invitation
    (B) Order a translation
    (C) Request an extension
    (D) Attend a party

38. Where are the speakers?
    (A) At an electronics store
    (B) At a parking garage
    (C) At an auto repair shop
    (D) At a coffee shop

39. What does the man say about his employees?
    (A) They are training now.
    (B) They will leave early today.
    (C) They work in pairs.
    (D) They are busy.

40. What is posted on a wall?
    (A) A password
    (B) A list of prices
    (C) A refund policy
    (D) A service agreement

41. What does the speakers' company produce?
    (A) Frozen vegetables
    (B) Biscuits
    (C) Juices
    (D) Breakfast cereals

42. What is the man concerned about?
    (A) Attracting new customers
    (B) Keeping a product fresh
    (C) Reducing environmental impact
    (D) Staying within a budget

43. Who will the speakers meet with next week?
    (A) A sales director
    (B) A marketing team
    (C) Some investors
    (D) Some store owners

GO ON TO THE NEXT PAGE ➡

TEST 1

44. According to the man, why is Alberto unavailable?

(A) He has left the company.
(B) He is meeting with a client.
(C) He is sick.
(D) He is on vacation.

45. What is the woman's job?

(A) Musician
(B) Caterer
(C) Event planner
(D) Photographer

46. What does the man remind the woman to do?

(A) Pick up some supplies
(B) Wear formal clothes
(C) Complete a checklist
(D) Keep some receipts

47. What did the board of directors most likely agree to do?

(A) Renovate an office space
(B) Hire some staff members
(C) Begin an advertising campaign
(D) Purchase better equipment

48. What did the man just receive?

(A) An employment contract
(B) A sales report
(C) Some logo designs
(D) Some shipping supplies

49. Why does the woman say, "I have to go to another meeting right now"?

(A) To decline an invitation
(B) To correct a misunderstanding
(C) To express excitement
(D) To explain a schedule change

50. What does the woman say she did recently?

(A) She moved to a new home.
(B) She opened a store.
(C) She planted a garden.
(D) She took a vacation.

51. What will the woman ask her friend for?

(A) A book about plants
(B) A flowerpot
(C) A pair of gloves
(D) A watering can

52. What will the woman most likely do on Saturday?

(A) Tour a park
(B) Go to a library
(C) Attend a workshop
(D) Watch a video

53. What industry do the speakers most likely work in?

(A) Publishing
(B) Entertainment
(C) Finance
(D) Fitness

54. What have the speakers volunteered to do?

(A) Distribute some books
(B) Speak at a local school
(C) Clean up a neighborhood park
(D) Advise community members

55. When will the man volunteer?

(A) In the morning
(B) During lunchtime
(C) In the afternoon
(D) In the evening

56. Where do the women most likely work?

(A) At a marketing firm
(B) At a hospital
(C) At a grocery store
(D) At a farm

57. Which of the man's qualifications is mentioned?

(A) His work experience
(B) His university degree
(C) His community service
(D) His writing ability

58. What will Jessica do?

(A) Provide training
(B) Arrange transportation
(C) Order equipment
(D) Lead a team project

---

59. What does the woman thank the man for doing?

(A) Hanging up some posters
(B) Organizing an event
(C) Repairing a machine
(D) Cooking a meal

60. Why does the woman say, "an Italian restaurant just opened nearby"?

(A) To complain about traffic
(B) To identify a job opportunity
(C) To extend an invitation
(D) To make a suggestion

61. What will the man send to a print shop?

(A) A schedule
(B) A map
(C) A company logo
(D) A list of sponsors

Promotion!

1 Shirt	5% off
2 Shirts	10% off
3 Shirts	20% off
4 Shirts	35% off

62. What does the man say he will do next week?

(A) Go on a trip
(B) Start a new job
(C) Attend a party
(D) Sign a contract

63. What does the man say he likes about a shirt?

(A) The color
(B) The fabric
(C) The style
(D) The length

64. Look at the graphic. What discount will the man receive on his purchase?

(A) 5%
(B) 10%
(C) 20%
(D) 35%

GO ON TO THE NEXT PAGE

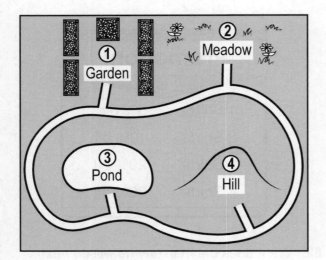

	Clay	-Low maintenance -Available in many colors
	Metal	-Durable -Easy installation
	Wood	-Lightweight -High quality
	Asphalt	-Affordable -Energy efficient

65. Who most likely are the speakers?

(A) Landscape designers
(B) Maintenance staff
(C) Security guards
(D) Forest rangers

66. Look at the graphic. Where will some work be done?

(A) In location 1
(B) In location 2
(C) In location 3
(D) In location 4

67. What will the speakers most likely do next?

(A) Obtain some cost estimates
(B) Take some photographs
(C) File a permit application
(D) Review an environmental study

68. According to the man, what recently happened?

(A) He moved into a new house.
(B) He received a pay raise.
(C) A storm damaged his roof.
(D) An addition was built on his home.

69. What does the man ask about?

(A) The cost of a service
(B) The length of a warranty
(C) The start date for a project
(D) The strength of a material

70. Look at the graphic. Which material will the man most likely select?

(A) Clay
(B) Metal
(C) Wood
(D) Asphalt

PART 4

Directions: You will hear some talks given by a single speaker. You will be asked to answer three questions about what the speaker says in each talk. Select the best response to each question and mark the letter (A), (B), (C), or (D) on your answer sheet. The talks will not be printed in your test book and will be spoken only one time.

71. What type of service is being advertised?
    (A) Cleaning
    (B) Interior decorating
    (C) Landscaping
    (D) Moving

72. What does the speaker say the company is proud of?
    (A) Its reasonable pricing
    (B) Its community programs
    (C) Its years of experience
    (D) The rewards it has received

73. What promotional offer does the speaker mention?
    (A) Free supplies
    (B) A free consultation
    (C) A discounted membership
    (D) A discounted hourly rate

74. Who most likely is the speaker?
    (A) A historian
    (B) A filmmaker
    (C) A factory owner
    (D) A tour guide

75. What industry does the speaker discuss?
    (A) Tea production
    (B) Magazine publishing
    (C) Tourism
    (D) Pottery manufacturing

76. What does the speaker encourage the listeners to do?
    (A) Take notes
    (B) Ask questions
    (C) View some objects
    (D) Purchase an item

77. What industry do the listeners most likely work in?
    (A) Entertainment
    (B) Manufacturing
    (C) Technology
    (D) Hospitality

78. What does the speaker imply when she says, "it was launched six months ago"?
    (A) A product will be discontinued.
    (B) A product became successful rapidly.
    (C) A product was released late.
    (D) A product is not well-known.

79. What is new about this year's conference?
    (A) It will be a three-day event.
    (B) It includes a contest for attendees.
    (C) It will not have on-site networking events.
    (D) It is not providing printed materials.

80. Who is the speaker?
    (A) A real estate agent
    (B) A shift manager
    (C) A company executive
    (D) A building inspector

81. What will happen to a building?
    (A) It will be expanded.
    (B) It will have its name changed.
    (C) It will be renovated.
    (D) It will be sold.

82. What should the listeners do by the end of this week?
    (A) Speak with a manager
    (B) Submit some photos
    (C) Provide some suggestions
    (D) Reply to an event invitation

GO ON TO THE NEXT PAGE

83. What products are being advertised?

(A) Outdoor furniture
(B) Camping supplies
(C) Gardening tools
(D) Bedroom furniture

84. What will Grove Emporium donate money to?

(A) A sports team
(B) A community theater
(C) An art museum
(D) A nature center

85. According to the speaker, why will an event not be held at the Greenville store?

(A) Renovations are taking place.
(B) Staff members are on vacation.
(C) Merchandise is sold out.
(D) Roads are under construction.

86. Who most likely are the listeners?

(A) Flight attendants
(B) Park rangers
(C) Warehouse workers
(D) Medical assistants

87. Why does the speaker say, "That's three times a day"?

(A) To question a new process
(B) To promote practicing a skill
(C) To clarify a responsibility
(D) To complain about a policy

88. What are the listeners asked to record in a logbook?

(A) Supply inventory
(B) Training hours
(C) Mechanical issues
(D) Driving distances

89. Who is Moritz Hoffman?

(A) An advertising executive
(B) An architect
(C) A city official
(D) A photographer

90. Why does the speaker say, "Moritz spent a great deal of time on preparation"?

(A) To recognize Moritz for his dedication
(B) To explain why Moritz was given a promotion
(C) To apologize for a project delay
(D) To suggest a change in work procedures

91. What will the listeners do next?

(A) Sign up for a newsletter
(B) Have refreshments
(C) Tour a worksite
(D) Watch a slideshow

92. What is the focus of the show?

(A) Gardening
(B) Baking
(C) Home repair
(D) Music

93. What does the speaker tell the listeners to do on a Web site?

(A) Sign up for a newsletter
(B) Download a document
(C) Upload a photograph
(D) Watch a video

94. According to the speaker, what did Heather Silva do this month?

(A) She moved to a new city.
(B) She went on tour.
(C) She opened a business.
(D) She published a book.

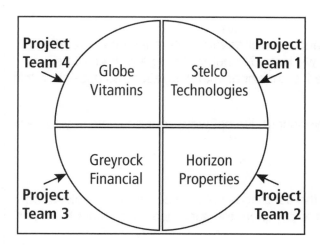

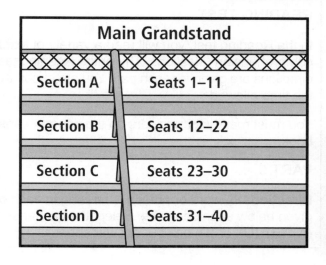

95. According to the speaker, what happened in March?

(A) A financial audit was conducted.
(B) An agency won an award.
(C) A company relocated its headquarters.
(D) A new policy was implemented.

96. What does the speaker announce about Scott Williams?

(A) He will be mentoring a new employee.
(B) He has been promoted to another position.
(C) He will be leaving the company.
(D) He will speak at a marketing conference.

97. Look at the graphic. Which additional team will Lauren be assigned to?

(A) Project Team 1
(B) Project Team 2
(C) Project Team 3
(D) Project Team 4

98. Why does the speaker say an event is special?

(A) A local team is playing in a championship game.
(B) Attendance reached a record high.
(C) It is the first game at a new stadium.
(D) It will be televised internationally.

99. Look at the graphic. Which section are the winners of the first prize seated in?

(A) Section A
(B) Section B
(C) Section C
(D) Section D

100. Why does the speaker recommend staying after the game?

(A) To tour a facility
(B) To meet team players
(C) To purchase souvenirs
(D) To watch some fireworks

This is the end of the Listening test. Turn to Part 5 in your test book.

READING TEST

In the Reading test, you will read a variety of texts and answer several different types of reading comprehension questions. The entire Reading test will last 75 minutes. There are three parts, and directions are given for each part. You are encouraged to answer as many questions as possible within the time allowed.

You must mark your answers on the separate answer sheet. Do not write your answers in your test book.

PART 5

Directions: A word or phrase is missing in each of the sentences below. Four answer choices are given below each sentence. Select the best answer to complete the sentence. Then mark the letter (A), (B), (C), or (D) on your answer sheet.

101. Starlight Noodle House ------- to open its first North American restaurant early next year.

    (A) plan
    (B) plans
    (C) planner
    (D) planning

102. For a small fee, Marvin's Fine Furniture will ------- items to customers' homes within two days of purchase.

    (A) deliver
    (B) sell
    (C) report
    (D) spend

103. There is no price ------- among Kalteco's three refrigerator models.

    (A) differ
    (B) different
    (C) difference
    (D) differently

104. McAlvey's Rental will provide the tents and seating needed ------- the upcoming festival.

    (A) against
    (B) near
    (C) into
    (D) for

105. Mr. Sorva handles all purchase orders ------- unless special approvals are needed.

    (A) he
    (B) him
    (C) his
    (D) himself

106. We appreciate your patience ------- our technology team works to restore the connection.

    (A) if
    (B) while
    (C) whether
    (D) but

107. Davison Avionics' sales department is ------- recruiting additional team members.

    (A) actively
    (B) active
    (C) activate
    (D) activity

108. It has been six months ------- Mr. Payne became president of Thornton Machinery.

    (A) since
    (B) from
    (C) where
    (D) between

109. The company has stayed profitable ------- by keeping operating costs low.

    (A) shortly
    (B) highly
    (C) mainly
    (D) greatly

110. Clients of Elise Salon receive text messages asking them to confirm their -------.

    (A) appoint
    (B) appointed
    (C) appointing
    (D) appointments

111. According to a *Consumer Now* poll, Bricktown Realty provides the ------- efficient real estate services in the area.

(A) very
(B) such
(C) quite
(D) most

112. Tolle Accounting's employee manual states that constructive disagreements are part of an ------- office culture.

(A) effect
(B) effects
(C) effective
(D) effectively

113. Marketing team members may work from home ------- they have their manager's permission.

(A) as long as
(B) as a result of
(C) depending on
(D) together with

114. The Petsonk Group is ------- to providing outstanding insurance at an affordable cost.

(A) reminded
(B) accepted
(C) required
(D) committed

115. The board of directors decided last night that Tina Chau should ------- as head of the legal department.

(A) continuous
(B) continue
(C) continued
(D) continuously

116. A large collection of bird fossils will be on display at the museum from May 15 ------- July 31.

(A) during
(B) until
(C) around
(D) throughout

117. Because so many members of the editorial staff use the printer, the office manager ------- has to order extra paper.

(A) frequency
(B) frequent
(C) frequenting
(D) frequently

118. Mr. Rhee thinks that the missing file is ------- in the archives.

(A) locating
(B) somewhere
(C) removed
(D) especially

119. Halle Theft Protection notifies customers immediately whenever there is a ------- of data security.

(A) breach
(B) contract
(C) secret
(D) reminder

120. The assembly instructions for the desk must be written very ------- to ensure that customers understand them.

(A) clearer
(B) clearest
(C) clears
(D) clearly

121. According to the *Baker Financial Journal*, investors' ------- for technology stocks rose sharply this quarter.

(A) enthusiasm
(B) enthusiast
(C) enthusiastic
(D) enthusiastically

122. All outerwear made by Arctic Hare is designed to withstand ------- cold temperatures.

(A) generously
(B) famously
(C) extremely
(D) suspiciously

GO ON TO THE NEXT PAGE →

TEST 1

123. ------- scheduling an examination at Central Wellness Clinic, clients will be asked a few health-related questions.

(A) Whereas
(B) When
(C) Although
(D) At

124. Owing to staff relocations, the company now has a ------- of office space at its headquarters.

(A) rate
(B) surplus
(C) factor
(D) profit

125. Having participated in ------- interviews during her job search, Ms. McKray expects that she will be hired soon.

(A) sizable
(B) countless
(C) plentiful
(D) much

126. Two prototypes of Viesso's mountain bike underwent user testing, and ------- were found to perform exceptionally well.

(A) less
(B) whose
(C) which
(D) both

127. ------- Ms. Uribe was promoted to director of development at Cranhurst International, she served in many other capacities.

(A) Before
(B) Instead
(C) Likewise
(D) Consequently

128. Landscape designers usually present several renderings to clients to help them ------- the completed project.

(A) appear
(B) resemble
(C) visualize
(D) express

129. ------- silk will be imported from Japan for our evening-wear fashion designs next season.

(A) Luxuriate
(B) Luxuriously
(C) Luxuries
(D) Luxurious

130. If its advertising revenue declines further, the magazine's future prospects are -------.

(A) reported
(B) insignificant
(C) uncertain
(D) overlooked

PART 6

Directions: Read the texts that follow. A word, phrase, or sentence is missing in parts of each text. Four answer choices for each question are given below the text. Select the best answer to complete the text. Then mark the letter (A), (B), (C), or (D) on your answer sheet.

Questions 131-134 refer to the following advertisement.

Commemorations Gifts

Is someone you know ------- an important birthday, anniversary, or graduation? Help them to mark
131.

the occasion with a unique present from Commemorations Gifts. We carry a large selection of

handmade items and art, including scented candles, jewelry, pottery, photographs, and paintings.

Shop online or visit ------- gallery to choose a one-of-a-kind work by a local artist. ------- .
132.   133.

We know it can be hard to choose the perfect gift, so we also offer digital gift cards in

denominations of $20 to $200. These have no expiration date and may be used online or in the

gallery, whichever is more ------- .
134.

131. (A) celebrate
(B) celebrating
(C) celebration
(D) celebrated

132. (A) your
(B) our
(C) their
(D) its

133. (A) It is important to acknowledge a
colleague's retirement.
(B) We are opening a second location in
the spring.
(C) Purchases can be shipped to any
address.
(D) Photography classes are offered in
the evenings.

134. (A) available
(B) qualified
(C) capable
(D) convenient

GO ON TO THE NEXT PAGE

Questions 135-138 refer to the following e-mail.

To: Wilson Jones <wjones@atterleyappliances.com>
From: Javi Preston <javipreston@yukoandjavisplace.com>
Date: April 22
Subject: Appliance delivery

Dear Mr. Jones:

I am sending this e-mail to ------- Atterley Appliances for your delivery service. It was excellent
                               135.
and exceeded my ------- in every way. My restaurant, Yuko and Javi's Place, is housed in a very
                  136.
old building with no elevator. The chest freezer I ordered from Atterley Appliances had to be

delivered to the building's top floor. ------- . It took careful maneuvering to avoid damaging the
                                        137.
stairway walls on the way up. Thanks to the team's patience and attention to detail, the new

freezer was installed with no damage to the ------- structure. Many thanks to Atterley Appliances
                                             138.
for your quality service.

Yours truly,

Javi Preston

---

135. (A) praise
     (B) reimburse
     (C) charge
     (D) forgive

136. (A) expects
     (B) expected
     (C) expecting
     (D) expectations

137. (A) The hallways are narrow, and the
         staircase is steep.
     (B) Our most popular dish is ramen, a
         traditional Japanese noodle soup.
     (C) Many chefs prefer to cook with gas.
     (D) We are registered with the local
         building preservation society.

138. (A) history
     (B) historic
     (C) historically
     (D) historian

Important Information from Well-Bright Electric

Well-Bright Electric is ------- a new billing system. During the setup period, customers will not be
        139.

able to access their accounts online. ------- . No late fees will be incurred for payments normally
                    140.

due on these dates. Please note that customers will ------- be able to contact the billing
                    141.

department during this time. However, ------- will have to call and speak to a representative
           142.

directly instead of using the online chat feature. All customers should rest assured that the new

billing system will enhance our customer service capabilities and allow us to provide bills that are

easier to view and understand.

---

139. (A) training
(B) investing
(C) promoting
(D) implementing

140. (A) We enjoy receiving notes from satisfied customers.
(B) The process will begin on May 2 and should be completed by May 21.
(C) Rates are expected to increase later this month.
(D) We are currently processing your request.

141. (A) still
(B) then
(C) moreover
(D) therefore

142. (A) we
(B) they
(C) mine
(D) yours

GO ON TO THE NEXT PAGE ➡

Questions 143-146 refer to the following article.

Marfisa Fashions Acquires Corvak Group

LOS ANGELES (May 11)—Marfisa Fashions, a leading designer of men's apparel, announced today that it has acquired the Tokyo-based Corvak Group. _____ . The news confirms speculation
143.
that Marfisa's executives _____ a company with robust distribution channels in Asia.
144.

"Corvak Group's reach in Asian markets will be a tremendous asset for us," said Jun-Young Min, Marfisa's CEO. "Our clients have been telling us for years that we need a stronger presence in Asia. _____ we are better able to meet their needs." While the press release did not specify the
145.
amount of the _____ , most analysts agree it was likely in the range of $100 to $150 million.
146.

---

143. (A) The deal was finalized last week.
    (B) Corvak Group's 600 employees are mostly full-time.
    (C) Marfisa Fashions will release its sales figures on Monday.
    (D) Men's denim pants are no longer in style.

144. (A) will pursue
    (B) pursuing
    (C) should have pursued
    (D) had been pursuing

145. (A) Otherwise
    (B) Now
    (C) Meanwhile
    (D) Already

146. (A) product
    (B) campaign
    (C) transaction
    (D) building

PART 7

Directions: In this part you will read a selection of texts, such as magazine and newspaper articles, e-mails, and instant messages. Each text or set of texts is followed by several questions. Select the best answer for each question and mark the letter (A), (B), (C), or (D) on your answer sheet.

Questions 147-148 refer to the following Web page.

https://www.lanolinfarm.com/info

Lanolin Farm—About Us

Lanolin Farm is home to two different breeds of sheep, each known for its unique characteristics. The first breed grows short, white wool that feels very soft. The other breed grows gray wool that is long and coarse. We shear the sheep twice a year to collect the wool.

Wool can be purchased from our farm store either as raw material or as yarn that we process on-site. The yarn can be used to make sweaters, hats, or blankets. We offer several colors of dyed wool as well as undyed wool that retains its natural color.

147. What is NOT mentioned as a characteristic of wool produced at the farm?
    (A) Color
    (B) Length
    (C) Texture
    (D) Strength

148. What is stated about the yarn sold by Lanolin Farm?
    (A) It is collected every two years.
    (B) It is prepared at a different farm.
    (C) It can be used to make various products.
    (D) It can be purchased only through mail order.

GO ON TO THE NEXT PAGE

Digital Tech Conference
May 15 and 16, 10:00 A.M.–5:00 P.M.
Exhibitor Information

Each exhibitor at the Digital Tech Conference will be allowed one booth space measuring 3 meters by 4 meters that includes two tables, four chairs, and access to electrical outlets. Exhibitors are responsible for supplying all other materials they may need.

Conference organizers will assign booth locations. The information will be e-mailed to exhibitors one week before the conference. A map of all exhibitors and their booth locations will be available on the conference Web site and at the conference itself.

Exhibitors may begin setting up their booths at 8:00 A.M. on May 15. All materials should be removed from booths by 7:00 P.M. on May 16.

During the conference, exhibitors must have at least one representative present at their booths at all times.

149. What will exhibitors receive in an e-mail?

   (A) Directions to the conference
   (B) An updated program
   (C) Booth location assignments
   (D) A map of the conference center

150. What are exhibitors required to do?

   (A) Maintain a presence in their booths
        throughout the conference
   (B) Finish setting up their booths by
        8:00 A.M. on May 15
   (C) Bring their own chairs and tables to
        the conference
   (D) Send an e-mail to conference
        organizers one week before the
        conference

TEST 1

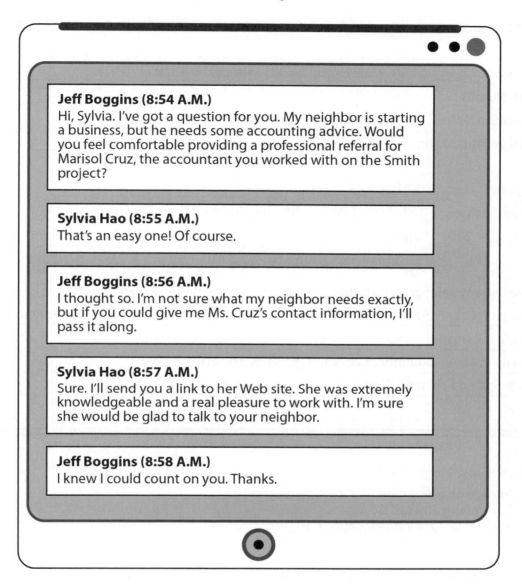

Jeff Boggins (8:54 A.M.)
Hi, Sylvia. I've got a question for you. My neighbor is starting a business, but he needs some accounting advice. Would you feel comfortable providing a professional referral for Marisol Cruz, the accountant you worked with on the Smith project?

Sylvia Hao (8:55 A.M.)
That's an easy one! Of course.

Jeff Boggins (8:56 A.M.)
I thought so. I'm not sure what my neighbor needs exactly, but if you could give me Ms. Cruz's contact information, I'll pass it along.

Sylvia Hao (8:57 A.M.)
Sure. I'll send you a link to her Web site. She was extremely knowledgeable and a real pleasure to work with. I'm sure she would be glad to talk to your neighbor.

Jeff Boggins (8:58 A.M.)
I knew I could count on you. Thanks.

151. Why did Mr. Boggins send a message to Ms. Hao?

(A) To ask whether she would recommend an accountant
(B) To highlight changes to a budget she prepared
(C) To give her his neighbor's contact information
(D) To provide her with feedback on a job candidate

152. At 8:55 A.M., what does Ms. Hao most likely mean when she writes, "That's an easy one"?

(A) She is free to meet with Mr. Boggins.
(B) She completed the Smith project quickly.
(C) She thinks Ms. Cruz would provide good advice.
(D) She believes that starting a business is a sensible decision.

GO ON TO THE NEXT PAGE ➡

Name:	Emma Megat
Address:	4 Exeter Road, #06-01, Singapore 182054
Phone Number:	+65 5557 0374
Application Date:	5 January
Available Start Date:	10 February

Company:	Nicoletta Skincare
Desired Position:	Manager, Visual Merchandising

Hours: X Full-time __ Days   Available weekends?

__ Part-time X Evenings   X Yes __ No

Please list any relevant educational or professional experience you have.

– Bachelor's degree in visual arts, specialisation in interior design, Freiburg Design College, Freiburg, Germany

– Nanala Fashion Boutique, London, UK, sales associate, 1 year

– Deep Spa and Fitness, Singapore, front desk associate, 8 months

153. Where is Ms. Megat applying to work?

(A) At Nicoletta Skincare
(B) At Freiburg Design College
(C) At Nanala Fashion Boutique
(D) At Deep Spa and Fitness

154. What can be concluded about Ms. Megat?

(A) She is interested in part-time employment.
(B) She prefers to work during the day.
(C) She has previous work experience as a manager.
(D) She has already held a job in Singapore.

Eurotrade Textile Magazine

AMSTERDAM (5 May)—Yesterday, the nonprofit organization Sustainable Textile Partnership, based in the Netherlands, released a report concerning the Turkish garment trade. It concludes that the Turkish garment industry could cut its annual spending by 18 percent by recycling cotton waste from its factories and fabric mills. The report was partially funded by the government of Turkey.

The Turkish garment industry imports thousands of metric tonnes of cotton a year. But it also throws away a mountain of cotton waste left over from sewn items. At present, some of this waste, including discarded fibres and leftover yarn, is used as filling for mattresses, but most of it is burned as rubbish. Recycling more of the scraps could reduce cotton imports and save substantial amounts of money, according to the partnership's report.

Onur Arslan, president of the Garment Manufacturers Association of Turkey, said, "Industry leaders are keenly interested in understanding the impacts of recycling."

155. The word "released" in paragraph 1, line 3, is closest in meaning to

(A) freed from
(B) made available
(C) abandoned
(D) fired

156. Who provided financial support for the Sustainable Textile Partnership report?

(A) A government
(B) An association
(C) A clothing manufacturer
(D) A recycling company

157. According to the article, what is done in Turkey with some cotton waste materials?

(A) They are made into low-quality cloth.
(B) They are used as mattress stuffing.
(C) They are recycled efficiently.
(D) They are donated to charitable organizations.

GO ON TO THE NEXT PAGE

Calling all amateur photographers!

Would you like to see your work featured in our magazine? Do you want to make an important statement about the environment? — [1] —.

Nurturing Nature magazine is holding a photography contest for our subscribers. All nonprofessional photographers are invited to submit up to five pictures illustrating their observations of the natural world. Photographs may be related to any of the following categories: the beauty of nature; people interacting with the natural world; and conservation activities. — [2] —. Submissions will be judged by the editors of *Nurturing Nature*, and all decisions are final. The top ten photographs will be featured in the May issue of the magazine. — [3] —.

Submissions are due by December 15. — [4] —. Additional information can be found on our Web site at www.nurturingnature.org/photo_contest.

---

158. For whom is the notice most likely intended?

(A) Contest judges
(B) Freelance writers
(C) Magazine subscribers
(D) Professional illustrators

159. What is NOT an acceptable subject for the contest photographs?

(A) A flower garden in bloom
(B) A child sitting in a classroom
(C) A snowstorm in the mountains
(D) A farmer planting grain in a field

160. In which of the positions marked [1], [2], [3], and [4] does the following sentence best belong?

"Moreover, the winning photograph will be shown on the magazine's cover."

(A) [1]
(B) [2]
(C) [3]
(D) [4]

```
╔══════════════════════════════════ *E-mail* ══════════════════════════════════╗
║                                                                                ║
║   To:          │ All Employees                                            │    ║
║                                                                                ║
║   From:        │ Ben Nonaka                                               │    ║
║                                                                                ║
║   Date:        │ March 22                                                 │    ║
║                                                                                ║
║   Subject:     │ Important information about time-tracking software       │    ║
║                                                                                ║
║   Hello, everyone,                                                             ║
║                                                                                ║
║   Please note that we will soon be retiring the Kronos time-tracking software, ║
║   as it has become too expensive for us to support two time-tracking programs. ║
║   Based on the usage data we collected from the survey you completed last week,║
║   we have decided to continue using only the software the employees like       ║
║   better. Using only the Workmine time-tracking software will allow us to       ║
║   provide better technical support and to maintain consistency in our records  ║
║   across the company.                                                          ║
║                                                                                ║
║   From April 4 to April 21, my department will offer training sessions on      ║
║   migrating records to the Workmine application. Kronos users should take      ║
║   advantage of this training, since they will not be able to access the Kronos ║
║   program after April 25. Starting on May 1, we will offer more-advanced       ║
║   Workmine training, including sessions on creating reports and troubleshooting.║
║   Please do not hesitate to contact me if you have questions or concerns about ║
║   this transition.                                                             ║
║                                                                                ║
║   Sincerely,                                                                   ║
║                                                                                ║
║   Ben Nonaka                                                                   ║
║   Director, Information Technology                                             ║
╚════════════════════════════════════════════════════════════════════════════════╝
```

161. According to the e-mail, why did the company choose Workmine over Kronos?

(A) Workmine is less expensive.
(B) Workmine uses new technology.
(C) Workmine produces clearer records.
(D) Workmine is preferred by employees.

162. What will be taught in the April training sessions?

(A) How to move data from one software program to another
(B) How to create advanced time-tracking reports
(C) How to collect data from employee surveys
(D) How to diagnose problems when using a software program

163. What is the first date when Kronos will no longer be available to employees?

(A) April 5
(B) April 22
(C) April 26
(D) May 2

GO ON TO THE NEXT PAGE

Hravn Announces Tour

LEEDS (17 May)—After a two-year break from touring, the Icelandic all-female band Hravn has announced an upcoming tour of the United Kingdom and Europe. — [1] —.

The band's Mystery Palace tour will begin in Leeds in the famed Victoria Garden before moving on to more than a dozen scheduled stops. The announcement was eagerly awaited by Hravn's many English fans, as the beloved rock band has recorded and released two new studio albums since it last went on tour. — [2] —.

The English rock band Wethersfield will be the opening act in the United Kingdom, but according to Dagur Arason, Hravn's tour manager, several other local rock music performers will open for the band at its European concerts. — [3] —.

Mr. Arason also confirmed that the band will soon be adding shows in North America. "I am negotiating with several venues in the United States and Canada right now," he said.

"I'm excited to get back on the road and connect with our fans in person," said lead guitarist Hallbera Lindarsdottir in a recent interview. "It will definitely be a show to remember!" — [4] —.

Tour dates are available on the band's Web site at www.hravn.is. Tickets can be purchased beginning on 22 June.

164. What is indicated in the article about the Victoria Garden?

(A) It is the studio where Hravn records its albums.

(B) It will be the first venue on Hravn's upcoming tour.

(C) It was once known as the Mystery Palace.

(D) It is the largest tour venue in the United Kingdom.

165. What can be concluded about Hravn?

(A) It plays traditional Icelandic folk music.

(B) It is not very popular in England.

(C) It made two albums during the last two years.

(D) It was formed two years ago in Leeds.

166. What is most likely true about Mr. Arason?

(A) He plays guitar for Wethersfield.

(B) He lives in Canada.

(C) He is married to Ms. Lindarsdottir.

(D) He schedules concerts for Hravn.

167. In which of the positions marked [1], [2], [3], and [4] does the following sentence best belong?

"She noted that the band has many new songs to share live for the first time."

(A) [1]

(B) [2]

(C) [3]

(D) [4]

Questions 168-171 refer to the following text-message chain.

> **Marvin Gartner (7:31 A.M.)**
> Hi, Simone and Julio. I'm picking up food for this morning's breakfast meeting. I got everything on the list except that special milk some people requested. Do you remember which kind? I should have written it down.
>
> **Simone Bonny (7:33 A.M.)**
> Whole milk and nonfat. A liter of each should be enough.
>
> **Marvin Gartner (7:34 A.M.)**
> I've got those. But some people prefer lactose-free milk. Was it soy milk? Oat milk? They have so many kinds here.
>
> **Julio Jimenez (7:40 A.M.)**
> Get almond milk. That was the consensus when I polled the team last week.
>
> **Simone Bonny (7:41 A.M.)**
> Never tried it. Do they have it, Marvin?
>
> **Julio Jimenez (7:42 A.M.)**
> It's tasty, low in fat, and high in protein.
>
> **Marvin Gartner (7:45 A.M.)**
> It's right here. Need anything else?
>
> **Simone Bonny (7:46 A.M.)**
> No. See you both at 8:30!

168. Why does Mr. Gartner begin the text-message chain?

(A) Because he wants to share some nutritional information

(B) Because he needs to know how many people will attend an event

(C) Because he might be late for a breakfast meeting

(D) Because he forgot to add an item to a list

169. Where most likely is Mr. Gartner?

(A) At a restaurant

(B) At a dairy farm

(C) In a grocery store

(D) In a meeting room

170. What can be concluded about Mr. Jimenez?

(A) He brought milk to the last team meeting.

(B) He needs more time to finalize a presentation.

(C) He asked coworkers about their milk preferences.

(D) He is a professional nutritionist.

171. At 7:41 A.M., what does Ms. Bonny imply when she writes, "Never tried it"?

(A) She drinks only nonfat milk.

(B) She is on a lactose-free diet.

(C) She does not think she would enjoy soy milk or oat milk.

(D) She does not know what almond milk tastes like.

GO ON TO THE NEXT PAGE

Copytrue Parts Service

If using classic older machinery in your manufacturing process is an integral part of your product's style and market identity, you know how frustrating it can be to try to find parts for equipment that has been in service for 50, 100, or 200 years or more. Don't let a broken part stop your production line and cut into your profits! Call Copytrue Parts Service. We are based in northern Massachusetts, with clients throughout Connecticut, New York, and Pennsylvania.

What we do
- We can use a broken part as a pattern and create a like-new intact replacement.
- Our machinists are avid experts in out-of-production and antique industrial equipment. They offer consulting services that will help you anticipate common breakages and get the parts you need before trouble starts.
- Our team can assess your company's maintenance routines and suggest improvements that will make old machinery last longer and function more efficiently.

We have worked on...
- metal presses and forges
- grain mills, waterwheels, and windmills
- industrial looms
- equipment made in England, Scotland, Ireland, France, Germany, Sweden, the United States, and other countries

Visit http://www.copytruepartsservice.com or call our main office at 978-555-0188 today!

172. Who are most likely to be clients of Copytrue Parts Service?

(A) Antiques collectors
(B) Factory owners
(C) Race car teams
(D) Aircraft designers

173. Where most likely is Copytrue Parts Service's main office?

(A) In Massachusetts
(B) In Connecticut
(C) In New York
(D) In Pennsylvania

174. What information is included in the advertisement?

(A) What brands are sold by the company
(B) The number of employees the company has
(C) The variety of services available from the company
(D) How long ago the company was founded

175. Why does the advertisement list several countries?

(A) To provide contact information for service representatives
(B) To identify the location of important customers
(C) To indicate where the staff received their training
(D) To emphasize the staff's knowledge and experience

GO ON TO THE NEXT PAGE

To:	Hinata Ishida <hishida91@lotuspond.net.jp>
From:	Guardos Insurance <customersupport@guardosinsurance.com.au>
Date:	8 April
Subject:	How did we do?

Dear Ms. Ishida,

Guardos Insurance appreciates its many loyal customers and would like to thank you for your trust in us. Since enrolling in our comprehensive motor vehicle insurance four years ago, you have saved an average of $510 per year compared to the cost of policies from leading competitors. Should you ever need insurance for your residence, for a commercial property, or for travel, we have great insurance products for these too.

Last week you contacted us to raise the liability coverage of your comprehensive motor vehicle insurance.

Because we value feedback from dedicated clients such as yourself, we would like to know your impression regarding the quality of service provided by our customer service agent Jillian Robins. Please take a minute to tell us how well Ms. Robins addressed your needs by completing the form at https://www.guardosinsurance.com.au/feedback.

Sincerely,

Alec Clarkson, Manager
Customer Assistance Team

---

https://www.guardosinsurance.com.au/feedback

Dear Valued Client: Please enter a brief description of your experience with our department in the following box.

> Guardos Insurance has been my insurer ever since my employer transferred me to Australia. I recently contacted your company to obtain advice about strengthening my liability coverage.
>
> Ms. Robins answered my questions and explained everything clearly. She mentioned that she is new to the position, however, so she put our phone chat on hold a couple of times while she checked on insurance coverage limits and terms. Ms. Robins was pleasant throughout our interaction. In the end, she helped me choose the insurance coverage that is appropriate for my needs, and I was pleased with her service.
>
> –Ms. Hinata Ishida

176. What is NOT included in the e-mail?

   (A) A list of services offered
   (B) An expression of gratitude
   (C) A discount offer on a policy
   (D) A request for customer feedback

177. Who most likely is Mr. Clarkson?

   (A) A corporate lawyer
   (B) An advertising executive
   (C) An insurance company owner
   (D) A customer service supervisor

178. In the e-mail, the word "impression" in paragraph 3, line 2, is closest in meaning to

   (A) mark
   (B) image
   (C) reaction
   (D) imitation

179. What can be concluded about Ms. Ishida?

   (A) She is planning to travel soon.
   (B) She relocated to Australia four years ago.
   (C) She is shopping for home insurance.
   (D) She had a different insurer during her first year in Australia.

180. What aspect of customer service did Ms. Robins have trouble with?

   (A) Product knowledge
   (B) Communication style
   (C) Patience with customers
   (D) Expertise with insurance software

GO ON TO THE NEXT PAGE

FROM	Laura Persaud Echelon International Hotel 120 East Street, Queenstown Georgetown, Guyana	**CUSTOMS DECLARATION** Origin: Georgetown, GY Shipping Date: 30 October
TO	Giles Hawkins 886 Main Street Edmonton, Alberta T5M 3K3 Canada	*Cleared Canada Customs 2 November*

Description of Contents	Quantity	Weight	Destination	Postage Fee
Excelsior Laptop Model RT3	1	1.8 kg	Zone 2	$7,500.00

Declaration of Exporter

I certify that the information on this form is correct and that the package does not contain dangerous or prohibited items.

Exporter's Signature:

Laura Persaud

To:	Alya Naimi <alya.naimi@echeloninternationalhotel.com>
From:	Giles Hawkins <ghawkins@drillritegeologicalservices.ca>
Date:	11 November
Subject:	Recovered laptop

Dear Ms. Naimi,

I stayed at the Echelon International Hotel in Georgetown, Guyana, on 28 October while attending a conference. After I checked out the next day, I realized I had mistakenly left my laptop behind. Apparently, I left it on the seat of the desk chair. I was supposed to travel to the Northwest Territories to do some geological research shortly after my return to Canada, and I desperately needed my laptop because I rely heavily on its geological mapping program.

I called the hotel from the Georgetown Airport and explained the problem to the manager, who immediately jumped into action. She personally arranged to have the laptop shipped to my company's headquarters in Canada via expedited delivery. Thanks to her quick action, I received it the same day that it cleared customs, and the following day I departed for the Northwest Territories. This display of guest-focused service is indicative of the high standard I have come to expect from the entire Echelon International chain. It is why your hotels are my first choice when I travel in Central and South America.

Sincerely,

Giles Hawkins
Lead Geologist, Drillrite Geological Services

181. What is suggested on the form?

(A) The item exceeded a weight limit.
(B) The item was shipped to Guyana.
(C) The package contained a computer.
(D) The package included a prohibited item.

182. What can be concluded about Ms. Persaud?

(A) She is the manager of a hotel.
(B) She recently purchased a laptop computer.
(C) She works for a company that exports electronics.
(D) She is a customs inspector in Canada.

183. Why did Mr. Hawkins write the e-mail?

(A) To thank an employee for making travel arrangements
(B) To offer praise for an employee's actions
(C) To inquire about an unexpected shipping charge
(D) To report that a hotel's computer has been damaged

184. When did Mr. Hawkins leave for the Northwest Territories?

(A) On October 28
(B) On October 29
(C) On November 2
(D) On November 3

185. In the e-mail, the word "standard" in paragraph 2, line 6, is closest in meaning to

(A) rule
(B) structure
(C) quality
(D) measure

GO ON TO THE NEXT PAGE

E-mail

To:	anchetagrill@worldmail.com
From:	maria.skrobol@granbyfilmfestival.com
Date:	February 15
Subject:	RE: Film festival dinner

Dear Mr. Ancheta,

Thank you for confirming that you can accommodate a party of 30 for the dinner on April 8. Before we can confirm the booking, I have a question about the sample menu you provided: Do you offer vegetarian dishes? We cannot book Ancheta Grill unless there are dining options for festival attendees who are vegetarians.

Many thanks,

Maria Skrobol

Granby Film Festival (April 6–9)
All events take place at Granby Cinema unless otherwise specified.

Thursday, April 6	Friday, April 7
Morning: Film screening of *Here, Now* (partly filmed in Granby) **Afternoon:** Walking tour of filming locations in Granby, led by Brandon Wang, the director of *Here, Now* **Evening:** Welcome party	**Morning:** Film screening of *La Vie* (in French with English subtitles) **Afternoon:** Panel discussion on films in translation **Evening:** Film screening: *Circles of Light*
Saturday, April 8	**Sunday, April 9**
Afternoon: Screening of finalists in the short-film competition; announcement of winners **Evening:** Festival dinner (location to be announced later)	**Afternoon:** Film screening of *Majesty* (followed by a question-and-answer session with *Majesty*'s director, Leticia Papineau) **Evening:** Farewell party

Granby Film Festival Registration Form

First name: Marco

Last name: Tai

E-mail: marcotai@jademail.com

Journalists: Check box to apply for free press pass. ☒

Days you will attend:

Thursday	$ 6	☐
Friday	$ 8	☒
Saturday	$10	☒
Sunday	$ 6	☐
Entire festival	$25	☐

Festival dinner at Ristorante Italia. Please note: only 30 spaces available, so book now.

Nonvegetarian	$12	☒
Vegetarian	$12	☐

Total cost: $30.00

---

186. Based on the e-mail, who most likely is Ms. Skrobol?

(A) The head chef at a restaurant
(B) A restaurant supply vendor
(C) The organizer of a festival
(D) A famous film critic

187. What can be concluded about Ancheta Grill?

(A) It was not available on April 8.
(B) It is located near Ristorante Italia.
(C) It cannot accommodate 30 people.
(D) It does not serve vegetarian options.

188. What is indicated on the schedule about all the films shown at the festival?

(A) They will be followed by panel discussions.
(B) They are French-language films.
(C) They will be shown at the same movie theater.
(D) They were directed by the same person.

189. What is indicated about Mr. Tai on the form?

(A) He works as a journalist.
(B) He will attend the entire festival.
(C) He is an experienced translator.
(D) He was unable to book a reservation for the festival dinner.

190. What event will Mr. Tai be able to attend?

(A) A tour of filming locations
(B) A short-film competition
(C) A farewell party
(D) A question-and-answer session with a director

GO ON TO THE NEXT PAGE ➡

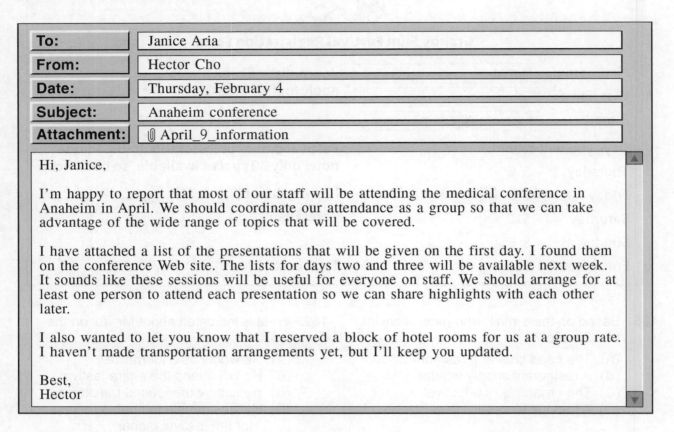

To:	Janice Aria
From:	Hector Cho
Date:	Thursday, February 4
Subject:	Anaheim conference
Attachment:	🔗 April_9_information

Hi, Janice,

I'm happy to report that most of our staff will be attending the medical conference in Anaheim in April. We should coordinate our attendance as a group so that we can take advantage of the wide range of topics that will be covered.

I have attached a list of the presentations that will be given on the first day. I found them on the conference Web site. The lists for days two and three will be available next week. It sounds like these sessions will be useful for everyone on staff. We should arrange for at least one person to attend each presentation so we can share highlights with each other later.

I also wanted to let you know that I reserved a block of hotel rooms for us at a group rate. I haven't made transportation arrangements yet, but I'll keep you updated.

Best,
Hector

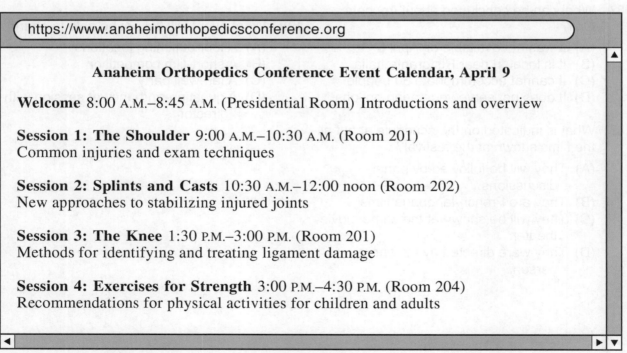

https://www.anaheimorthopedicsconference.org

Anaheim Orthopedics Conference Event Calendar, April 9

Welcome 8:00 A.M.–8:45 A.M. (Presidential Room) Introductions and overview

Session 1: The Shoulder 9:00 A.M.–10:30 A.M. (Room 201)
Common injuries and exam techniques

Session 2: Splints and Casts 10:30 A.M.–12:00 noon (Room 202)
New approaches to stabilizing injured joints

Session 3: The Knee 1:30 P.M.–3:00 P.M. (Room 201)
Methods for identifying and treating ligament damage

Session 4: Exercises for Strength 3:00 P.M.–4:30 P.M. (Room 204)
Recommendations for physical activities for children and adults

To:	Hector Cho
From:	Janice Aria
Date:	Friday, February 5
Subject:	RE: Anaheim conference

Hector,

I like your suggestion of coordinating our conference attendance. I can create an informal sign-up document so that everyone can get an idea of what sessions are available and we can make sure we cover all of them.

I appreciate the information from the Web site. I didn't know it was already available. I definitely want to attend the session on dealing with ligament injuries. Once we get the schedule for the additional conference sessions, I'll send it out to the team, together with the attendance sign-up sheet.

It's great that you were able to get that group discount. Conferences like this are a big expense, but your efforts will certainly save us money.

Thanks,

Janice

191. In the first e-mail, what information does Mr. Cho provide in the attachment?

(A) A list of employees invited to a conference
(B) An agenda showing some presentation topics
(C) Recommendations for restaurants in Anaheim
(D) Suggestions to increase conference attendance

192. What field do Ms. Aria and Mr. Cho most likely work in?

(A) Health care
(B) Human resources
(C) Travel
(D) Law

193. In the second e-mail, what does Ms. Aria offer to do?

(A) Sign a contract with a conference organizer
(B) Consult a specialist for advice
(C) Ask employees for their opinions
(D) Create a document to organize attendance

194. What session is Ms. Aria most interested in attending?

(A) Session 1
(B) Session 2
(C) Session 3
(D) Session 4

195. In the second e-mail, what discounted cost does Ms. Aria refer to?

(A) Rental cars
(B) Hotel rates
(C) Plane tickets
(D) Conference fees

GO ON TO THE NEXT PAGE

An Unexpected Plot Twist for a Seasoned Mystery Novelist

Fans of Delia Ramiro's mystery novels may be surprised when opening her new book. While Ms. Ramiro's novels usually feature crafty detectives and suspenseful plots interwoven with lengthy descriptions of mouthwatering meals, *The Vanishing Plate* is all about the recipes.

This attractive cookbook gives detailed instructions for making the many dishes featured in Ms. Ramiro's fiction, such as the lentil soup served by Derek Donne at the end of *The Alpine Enigma*, the debut novel that was published while Ms. Ramiro was still a university student.

"My literary agent, Bernice Holm, wanted me to write another international thriller," Ms. Ramiro said recently in an interview. "But readers kept asking me about the cuisine in my novels. They wanted to know how they could make it themselves!"

For Ms. Ramiro, the new book is not as big a departure as it may seem.

"As a child, I read cookbooks like they were novels," she said. "For me back then, *The Saffron Table* was as exciting as any adventure story."

When asked whether she expects the new book to be as successful as her previous one, *The Garnet Butterfly*, Ms. Ramiro had a quick answer.

"It may not sell as many copies, but people will want to keep it for years," she said. "The images in the book are works of art all on their own. Even if you don't make my version of chocolate soufflé, you'll be enchanted by the photograph of it."

The Vanishing Plate by Delia Ramiro. 300 pages. Sand Street Publishing. $50.

---

https://www.thebooknews.com/reviews/20sept/vanishing_plate

Hudson Keita Reviews *The Vanishing Plate*

It would seem that everyone is a chef these days. So far this year no fewer than 20 cookbooks by celebrities—actors, writers, and athletes—have hit bookstore shelves. Fortunately, Delia Ramiro's *The Vanishing Plate* is one of those rare celebrity cookbooks that can hold its own alongside those by professional chefs. This handsomely produced volume, featuring photographs by Selda Solberg and a foreword by award-winning chef Lukas Fogt, features over 100 creative and tantalizing recipes. Despite the puzzling title, the recipes themselves are clearly written and generously detailed. If only the book were not priced so exorbitantly ($50 for a cookbook?), I would say that it should become a staple in the kitchen of every home cook.

THE SOUTHWESTERNER MONTHLY

Book Review: Delia Ramiro's *The Vanishing Plate*

Delia Ramiro's *The Vanishing Plate* is not for the faint of heart. Inspired by scenes in the novelist's acclaimed mysteries and thrillers, the recipes are significantly more complicated than those in your typical gourmet cookbook. Most of Ramiro's recipes assume the reader is proficient in mid-level cooking techniques, and a few recipes would likely be attempted only by cooks with professional experience. If you are the ideal reader who is up to the challenge, however, the book will not disappoint you. All the recipes are innovative—not one failed to surprise me in one way or another—and they produce dishes that I believe would impress even the most discriminating diner. That said, the book is not without its faults. In addition to a hefty price tag, it devotes too much space to the history of the ingredients. While such information can be interesting, I would have preferred a trimmer, more concise book that showcases the recipes themselves and is easier to handle in the kitchen.

—Paulina Yu

196. According to the first review, how does Ms. Ramiro's new book differ from her previous ones?

(A) It is significantly longer.
(B) It is a different type of book.
(C) It is in a different language.
(D) It was written with a coauthor.

197. In the first review, what book is mentioned as the first novel written by Ms. Ramiro?

(A) *The Vanishing Plate*
(B) *The Alpine Enigma*
(C) *The Saffron Table*
(D) *The Garnet Butterfly*

198. Whose work does Ms. Ramiro praise in an interview?

(A) Derek Donne's
(B) Bernice Holm's
(C) Selda Solberg's
(D) Lukas Fogt's

199. According to the third review, who are the ideal readers for Ms. Ramiro's new book?

(A) People who are professional writers themselves
(B) People who have read Ms. Ramiro's previous books
(C) People who read books to find creative inspiration
(D) People who have mastered a specific set of skills

200. What do Mr. Keita and Ms. Yu both consider to be a problem with Ms. Ramiro's new book?

(A) Its high price
(B) Its confusing title
(C) Its focus on ingredients
(D) Its factual errors

Stop! This is the end of the test. If you finish before time is called, you may go back to Parts 5, 6, and 7 and check your work.

NO TEST MATERIAL ON THIS PAGE

TEST 2

 **150-231**

LISTENING TEST ⋯⋯⋯⋯⋯⋯⋯⋯⋯⋯⋯⋯ p.72

READING TEST ⋯⋯⋯⋯⋯⋯⋯⋯⋯⋯⋯⋯⋯ p.84

＊解答用紙は本冊 p.112 の後ろに綴じ込まれています。

実際のテストでは問題用紙の裏側に、以下のようなテスト全体についての指示が印刷されています。
この指示を念頭において、テストに取り組みましょう。

General Directions

This test is designed to measure your English language ability. The test is divided into two sections: Listening and Reading.

You must mark all of your answers on the separate answer sheet. For each question, you should select the best answer from the answer choices given. Then, on your answer sheet, you should find the number of the question and fill in the space that corresponds to the letter of the answer that you have selected. If you decide to change an answer, completely erase your old answer and then mark your new answer.

訳　　　　　　　　　　**全体についての指示**

このテストはあなたの英語言語能力を測定するよう設計されています。テストはリスニングとリーディングという
2 つのセクションに分けられています。

答えは全て別紙の解答用紙にマークしてください。それぞれの設問について、与えられた選択肢から最も適切な答え
を選びます。そして解答用紙の該当する設問番号に、選択した答えを塗りつぶしてください。答えを修正する場合は、
元の答えを完全に消してから新しい答えをマークしてください。

LISTENING TEST

In the Listening test, you will be asked to demonstrate how well you understand spoken English. The entire Listening test will last approximately 45 minutes. There are four parts, and directions are given for each part. You must mark your answers on the separate answer sheet. Do not write your answers in your test book.

PART 1

Directions: For each question in this part, you will hear four statements about a picture in your test book. When you hear the statements, you must select the one statement that best describes what you see in the picture. Then find the number of the question on your answer sheet and mark your answer. The statements will not be printed in your test book and will be spoken only one time.

Statement (C), "They're sitting at a table," is the best description of the picture, so you should select answer (C) and mark it on your answer sheet.

1.

2.

GO ON TO THE NEXT PAGE ➡

3.

4.

5.

TEST 2

6.

GO ON TO THE NEXT PAGE

PART 2

Directions: You will hear a question or statement and three responses spoken in English. They will not be printed in your test book and will be spoken only one time. Select the best response to the question or statement and mark the letter (A), (B), or (C) on your answer sheet.

7. Mark your answer on your answer sheet.

8. Mark your answer on your answer sheet.

9. Mark your answer on your answer sheet.

10. Mark your answer on your answer sheet.

11. Mark your answer on your answer sheet.

12. Mark your answer on your answer sheet.

13. Mark your answer on your answer sheet.

14. Mark your answer on your answer sheet.

15. Mark your answer on your answer sheet.

16. Mark your answer on your answer sheet.

17. Mark your answer on your answer sheet.

18. Mark your answer on your answer sheet.

19. Mark your answer on your answer sheet.

20. Mark your answer on your answer sheet.

21. Mark your answer on your answer sheet.

22. Mark your answer on your answer sheet.

23. Mark your answer on your answer sheet.

24. Mark your answer on your answer sheet.

25. Mark your answer on your answer sheet.

26. Mark your answer on your answer sheet.

27. Mark your answer on your answer sheet.

28. Mark your answer on your answer sheet.

29. Mark your answer on your answer sheet.

30. Mark your answer on your answer sheet.

31. Mark your answer on your answer sheet.

PART 3

Directions: You will hear some conversations between two or more people. You will be asked to answer three questions about what the speakers say in each conversation. Select the best response to each question and mark the letter (A), (B), (C), or (D) on your answer sheet. The conversations will not be printed in your test book and will be spoken only one time.

32. What was recently built?
    (A) A restaurant
    (B) A hotel
    (C) An airport
    (D) A parking area

33. According to the woman, what will customers like about a service?
    (A) It will be environmentally friendly.
    (B) It will be available 24 hours a day.
    (C) It will not require reservations.
    (D) It will be free of charge.

34. What does the man ask the woman to do?
    (A) Gather some information
    (B) Train some staff
    (C) Clean some vehicles
    (D) Apply for a permit

35. Why does the man contact the woman?
    (A) To get directions to her office
    (B) To offer her a job
    (C) To arrange for a meeting
    (D) To purchase a newspaper subscription

36. What does the man say will take place next week?
    (A) A grand-opening event
    (B) A product launch
    (C) A retirement party
    (D) A career fair

37. What does the woman ask permission to do?
    (A) Postpone a subscription
    (B) Park in a certain area
    (C) Call some references
    (D) Take pictures

38. What is the man organizing?
    (A) A fund-raising event
    (B) A community festival
    (C) A company retreat
    (D) A professional conference

39. What idea does the woman say she likes?
    (A) Giving away free samples
    (B) Providing a shuttle service
    (C) Offering group activities
    (D) Inviting a guest speaker

40. What does the man decide to do next?
    (A) Plan a menu
    (B) Make a payment
    (C) Call a city office
    (D) Hire a cleaning service

41. Where is the conversation most likely taking place?
    (A) At a textile factory
    (B) At a grocery store
    (C) At a bakery
    (D) At a food manufacturing plant

42. What does the man mean when he says, "I saw the truck leave about an hour ago"?
    (A) A delivery was not made.
    (B) A truck driver left without the woman.
    (C) A product should now be available.
    (D) A supplier filled an order incorrectly.

43. Why did the woman e-mail the man yesterday?
    (A) To invite him to a training event
    (B) To apply for a new position
    (C) To ask for vacation time
    (D) To make a complaint

GO ON TO THE NEXT PAGE ➡

TEST 2

44. Where is the conversation taking place?

(A) At a hotel
(B) At a restaurant
(C) At an art gallery
(D) At a concert hall

45. Who does the woman say gave her some instructions?

(A) Her client
(B) Her manager
(C) An event planner
(D) An interior designer

46. What does the man agree to do?

(A) Sell some tickets
(B) Take an extra work shift
(C) Cancel a reservation
(D) Take care of a group of people

47. Where do the speakers most likely work?

(A) At an automobile manufacturer
(B) At a cosmetics developer
(C) At a construction firm
(D) At a technology company

48. Why was a business trip canceled?

(A) A client ended a contract.
(B) A supplier will be replaced.
(C) A flaw in a product was discovered.
(D) A flight was canceled.

49. What does the woman say she will do?

(A) Contact a travel agent
(B) Review some presentation slides
(C) Apply for more funding
(D) Revise an instruction manual

50. What problem does the woman mention?

(A) A source of funding has been lost.
(B) An entertainer is not available.
(C) Bad weather is predicted.
(D) A permit has not been approved.

51. Where did the woman go this morning?

(A) To a community center
(B) To a bank
(C) To a music shop
(D) To a bookstore

52. What will Roberto most likely do after the meeting?

(A) Call his brother
(B) Check his e-mail
(C) Visit a Web site
(D) Adjust a budget

53. Why is So-Hyoon nervous?

(A) She has participated only in smaller productions.
(B) She has a lot of lines to remember.
(C) She has to sing a solo.
(D) She has not yet met the other cast members.

54. What does the man say he will give to So-Hyoon?

(A) A parking pass
(B) A notebook
(C) A schedule
(D) A room number

55. Why does Shreya interrupt the conversation?

(A) To start a rehearsal
(B) To provide a backstage tour
(C) To arrange for a photoshoot
(D) To take costume measurements

56. Where do the speakers most likely work?

(A) At an advertising agency
(B) At a training consultancy
(C) At a law firm
(D) At a social media company

57. What does the man offer to do?

(A) Review a contract
(B) Purchase some advertising space
(C) Lead a project
(D) Contact Human Resources

58. What will the man do next?

(A) Assemble a team
(B) Write an online review
(C) Negotiate a higher salary
(D) Conduct some research

---

59. Where is the conversation most likely taking place?

(A) At an art supply store
(B) At a furniture outlet
(C) At a car dealership
(D) At a sporting goods shop

60. Why is the woman concerned?

(A) She lost her wallet.
(B) A product is damaged.
(C) A color is not available.
(D) A warranty is not included.

61. Why does the woman say, "Thursday is two days from now"?

(A) To express surprise
(B) To make a correction
(C) To offer reassurance
(D) To show disappointment

October Class Schedule		
Mon.	5:00 P.M.	Vegetarian Delights
Tues.	6:30 P.M.	Intro to Pasta Making
Wed.	7:00 P.M.	Bread Making for Beginners
Thurs.	4:30 P.M.	Advanced Bread Making
Fri.	5:30 P.M.	Classic French Cuisine

62. How did the man first learn about a program?

(A) From the radio
(B) From a newspaper
(C) From a neighbor
(D) From a Web site

63. Look at the graphic. What course will the man sign up for?

(A) Vegetarian Delights
(B) Intro to Pasta Making
(C) Bread Making for Beginners
(D) Advanced Bread Making

64. What does the woman want the man to do?

(A) Speak to an instructor
(B) Purchase class materials
(C) Pay with a credit card
(D) Fill out a survey

TEST 2

Item	Quantity
Business cards	100
Exhibit banners	10
Brochures	75
Posters	50

Filter Model	Price
J3	$26
T5	$32
X7	$55
Y12	$70

65. What industry do the speakers most likely work in?

(A) Art
(B) Entertainment
(C) Catering
(D) Technology

66. Look at the graphic. Which item arrived in the wrong quantity?

(A) Business cards
(B) Exhibit banners
(C) Brochures
(D) Posters

67. What is the man concerned about?

(A) A deadline
(B) Paper quality
(C) A venue
(D) An extra expense

68. According to the woman, what is wrong with the water in the pool?

(A) It is cloudy.
(B) It is too cold.
(C) It has a bad smell.
(D) It contains too many chemicals.

69. Look at the graphic. How much will a replacement part cost?

(A) $26
(B) $32
(C) $55
(D) $70

70. What will the man most likely do later today?

(A) Submit an invoice
(B) Clean some equipment
(C) Post an announcement
(D) Visit a store

PART 4

Directions: You will hear some talks given by a single speaker. You will be asked to answer three questions about what the speaker says in each talk. Select the best response to each question and mark the letter (A), (B), (C), or (D) on your answer sheet. The talks will not be printed in your test book and will be spoken only one time.

71. What does the speaker feel proud about?
    (A) A hiring decision
    (B) A company's expansion
    (C) An industry award
    (D) A project's completion

72. According to product reviews, what did customers like most about a product?
    (A) The affordable price
    (B) The storage capability
    (C) The stylish design
    (D) The ease of operation

73. How will a product most likely change?
    (A) Digital controls will be added.
    (B) More colors will be offered.
    (C) Stronger materials will be used.
    (D) Adjustable shelves will be installed.

74. Where is the announcement most likely taking place?
    (A) At a ferry station
    (B) At an airport
    (C) At a train depot
    (D) At a taxi stand

75. What will some of the listeners receive?
    (A) A schedule
    (B) A refund
    (C) A food voucher
    (D) An identification badge

76. What does the speaker remind the listeners about?
    (A) Luggage restrictions
    (B) Safety procedures
    (C) Entertainment options
    (D) Building hours

77. Where does the speaker most likely work?
    (A) At a university
    (B) At a technology firm
    (C) At a magazine publisher
    (D) At a public library

78. Why does the speaker say, "there's an error message when I try to download the files"?
    (A) To give an excuse
    (B) To request assistance
    (C) To express caution
    (D) To correct a misunderstanding

79. What does the speaker tell the listener to do?
    (A) Prepare for a discussion
    (B) Contact a computer store
    (C) Reprint some articles
    (D) Stop some research

80. Who is the speaker?
    (A) A sales representative
    (B) A store manager
    (C) A company executive
    (D) A news reporter

81. What type of product does the company make?
    (A) Vehicles
    (B) Furniture
    (C) Dishware
    (D) Electronics

82. What will happen next?
    (A) Some instructions will be given.
    (B) Some uniforms will be distributed.
    (C) Some questions will be collected.
    (D) Some materials will be unpacked.

GO ON TO THE NEXT PAGE ➡

TEST 2

83. What is the speaker calling about?

(A) Car maintenance
(B) Boat renovations
(C) Park development
(D) Home repairs

84. What does the speaker imply when he says, "we have several new crew members on the project"?

(A) The payroll needs to be updated.
(B) The crew's work is impressive.
(C) A requested due date cannot be met.
(D) Some colleagues will need driving directions.

85. What will the listener receive this afternoon?

(A) An inspection report
(B) Some photographs
(C) An invoice
(D) A delivery

86. What does the speaker say the company is passionate about?

(A) Keeping the oceans clean
(B) Reducing waste in landfills
(C) Stopping air pollution
(D) Preserving forests

87. According to the speaker, what does the company collect?

(A) Plastic packaging
(B) Soil samples
(C) Cash donations
(D) Electronic devices

88. What does the speaker say the listeners can request?

(A) A receipt
(B) A tour of a site
(C) A shipping label
(D) A free guidebook

89. Where are the listeners?

(A) In a sports arena
(B) In a theater
(C) In a classroom
(D) In a bookstore

90. Why does the speaker praise some students?

(A) Their financial goals were met.
(B) Their project received many positive reviews.
(C) They solved a problem quickly.
(D) They dedicated a lot of time to a project.

91. What does the speaker ask the listeners to do?

(A) Take their seats
(B) Gather in the lobby
(C) Enjoy some refreshments
(D) Silence electronic devices

92. Where does the speaker work?

(A) At an architectural firm
(B) At a historical foundation
(C) At a construction company
(D) At a concert hall

93. Why does the speaker say, "I just heard that there is fog at the airport"?

(A) To suggest using alternate transportation
(B) To request help from the audience
(C) To explain a schedule change
(D) To complain about poor communication

94. Who does the speaker thank at the end of the speech?

(A) An archivist
(B) An event planner
(C) Some public officials
(D) Some restaurant owners

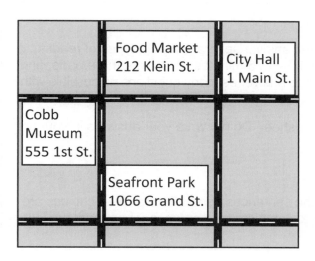

Project Step	Beginning Date
Model development	July 27
Client review	August 3
Prototype revisions	August 8
Production	August 16

95. What aspect of the city will the listeners learn about on the tour?

(A) Its industries
(B) Its history
(C) Its art
(D) Its parks

96. According to the speaker, what is included in the tickets?

(A) Meal discounts
(B) Free parking
(C) Complimentary photographs
(D) Museum admission

97. Look at the graphic. Where will the tour end?

(A) At 212 Klein St.
(B) At 1 Main St.
(C) At 1066 Grand St.
(D) At 555 1st St.

98. Where does the speaker work?

(A) At a glass factory
(B) At an interior design firm
(C) At a perfume developer
(D) At a cosmetics store

99. Look at the graphic. By which date is the listener asked to complete a project?

(A) July 27
(B) August 3
(C) August 8
(D) August 16

100. What does the speaker say she will pay for?

(A) Additional materials
(B) Legal fees
(C) Expedited service
(D) Staff training

This is the end of the Listening test. Turn to Part 5 in your test book.

GO ON TO THE NEXT PAGE

TEST 2

READING TEST

In the Reading test, you will read a variety of texts and answer several different types of reading comprehension questions. The entire Reading test will last 75 minutes. There are three parts, and directions are given for each part. You are encouraged to answer as many questions as possible within the time allowed.

You must mark your answers on the separate answer sheet. Do not write your answers in your test book.

PART 5

Directions: A word or phrase is missing in each of the sentences below. Four answer choices are given below each sentence. Select the best answer to complete the sentence. Then mark the letter (A), (B), (C), or (D) on your answer sheet.

101. The new microwave for the office kitchen should arrive ------- the week.

(A) on
(B) along
(C) by
(D) within

102. Mr. Samudio thanked the hotel staff for making ------- stay a comfortable one.

(A) he
(B) his
(C) him
(D) himself

103. The sales associates have been pleased with the new dress code ------- it was implemented last September.

(A) here
(B) first
(C) since
(D) best

104. At the beginning of the class, your instructor will inform you ------- additional materials are needed.

(A) yet
(B) if
(C) however
(D) although

105. Poole and Whitney Supply sells premier products for do-it-yourself home improvement -------.

(A) projects
(B) projection
(C) projecting
(D) projectors

106. Mouse pads ------- our redesigned company logo will be distributed after the workshop.

(A) must display
(B) to be displayed
(C) displaying
(D) being displayed

107. Employees who work part-time are not ------- for the company's profit-sharing plan.

(A) famous
(B) admired
(C) reasonable
(D) eligible

108. Brady Music Academy pairs students with qualified instructors ------- are professional wind and brass instrument players.

(A) who
(B) when
(C) where
(D) whose

109. Residents of Millier Street ------- city council members to approve the installation of a traffic light.

(A) encouraged
(B) suggested
(C) argued
(D) reported

110. At the meeting tomorrow, Jing Huang, vice president of sales, will discuss the company's ------- to achieve its sales goals.

(A) effortless
(B) efforts
(C) effortful
(D) effortlessly

111. Chef Ferguson ------- mixed the spices during her cooking demonstration.

(A) extremely
(B) expertly
(C) tightly
(D) finely

112. To receive a parking pass, you must submit a ------- request to your supervisor.

(A) formalize
(B) formally
(C) formality
(D) formal

113. The customer survey results show that there are ------- issues that need to be addressed.

(A) faithful
(B) numerous
(C) classical
(D) rapid

114. Ms. Liu requested that her mail be ------- to the New York office during the month of June.

(A) forward
(B) forwards
(C) forwarded
(D) forwarding

115. Supeck Legal is closed while the sprinkler system is being replaced ------- the building.

(A) into
(B) to
(C) throughout
(D) among

116. Gabary Ltd. decided to expand its marketing staff, so salaries for newly hired employees are ------- high.

(A) reasonably
(B) reasonable
(C) reasons
(D) reasoned

117. Ms. Baek needs to sign the standard ------- to start working as an operations consultant.

(A) reference
(B) advice
(C) format
(D) agreement

118. Companies relocating ------- headquarters to Burton County must submit a proposed timeline for the move.

(A) them
(B) their
(C) themselves
(D) theirs

119. Although a date has not been -------, the Culvert Silver Line is expected to resume operations next year.

(A) positioned
(B) perfected
(C) specified
(D) amplified

120. Operating at a ------- of 100 sheets per minute, the Nobia XLR is one of the fastest photocopiers on the market.

(A) period
(B) rate
(C) distance
(D) page

GO ON TO THE NEXT PAGE

121. Dr. Cheon is ------- reluctant to accept new patients at this time given his current caseload.

(A) understandably
(B) understandable
(C) understanding
(D) understood

122. ------- customer will receive a free gift with any purchase at Trayton Tools on its opening day.

(A) Certain
(B) All
(C) Few
(D) Each

123. The Elevpro jacket features an adjustable hood for extra ------- against cold weather.

(A) protect
(B) protection
(C) protector
(D) protected

124. The reforestation plan is proceeding smoothly, although the organizers ------- some minor issues in the early stages.

(A) concluded
(B) accomplished
(C) earned
(D) encountered

125. The institute's directors have decided to reinvest the budget surplus ------- spending the extra money.

(A) instead of
(B) paid for
(C) apart from
(D) offers to

126. The clients could not agree on contract wording, and unfortunately, ------- could the lawyers.

(A) perhaps
(B) meanwhile
(C) neither
(D) rather

127. References must be ------- by a human resources specialist before a job candidate arrives for an interview.

(A) verifying
(B) verifies
(C) verified
(D) verification

128. Mr. Lee ended the department meeting ------- in order to greet a prominent client.

(A) hardly
(B) widely
(C) immensely
(D) abruptly

129. The accounting software has been developed in an ------- fashion over the past two years.

(A) increment
(B) incrementally
(C) increments
(D) incremental

130. The document outlines possible ------- of building without a permit in the municipality.

(A) adjustments
(B) consequences
(C) alignments
(D) designs

PART 6

Directions: Read the texts that follow. A word, phrase, or sentence is missing in parts of each text. Four answer choices for each question are given below the text. Select the best answer to complete the text. Then mark the letter (A), (B), (C), or (D) on your answer sheet.

Questions 131-134 refer to the following instructions.

Before replacing a cracked screen on a customer's mobile phone, always examine the phone thoroughly to identify additional issues, cosmetic or otherwise. This ------- will ensure that we will
                                                                                         131.
not be held responsible for a feature that was already flawed. If you detect evidence of corrosion

or moisture, make a note of it. ------- . Also, make sure to check the key components.
                                 132.

------- include the headphone jack, the microphone, the flashlight, the camera, and the volume
133.

controls. A checklist is available to guide you ------- the process.
                                               134.

131. (A) device
     (B) individual
     (C) inspection
     (D) skill

132. (A) We will contact the customer soon.
     (B) This is likely a sign of water damage.
     (C) Hold the button down for five seconds.
     (D) The two pieces may not be missing.

133. (A) Others
     (B) Whichever
     (C) Many
     (D) These

134. (A) onto
     (B) under
     (C) beyond
     (D) through

GO ON TO THE NEXT PAGE

SEOUL (19 August)—Korean carmaker Hwan Automotive has announced the release of its first all-electric vehicle in North America. The Nalgae electric vehicle ------- available in Hwan Automotive showrooms in the United States and Canada beginning in May of next year. The Nalgae has been on the market in Asia for more than two years. ------- will continue to be manufactured in Seoul while a new assembly plant is built in Calgary. A dedicated battery manufacturing complex is also slated for construction near the plant. -------. Residents are looking forward to this development.

135.

136.

137.

"This is our biggest ------- ever outside of Asia," stated Hwan Automotive CEO Do-Yun Park. "We are very excited about introducing the Nalgae to the North American market."

138.

135. (A) will be
(B) can be
(C) was going to be
(D) would have been

136. (A) It
(B) Both
(C) Either
(D) Those

137. (A) A prototype vehicle was on exhibit at the Beijing car show last year.
(B) Hwan Automotive has won awards for its innovative technology.
(C) Premium options are available at additional cost.
(D) Altogether, the expansion is expected to create 5,500 new jobs.

138. (A) promotion
(B) investment
(C) celebration
(D) performance

To: Lucinda Richards <lrichards@mailcrate.co.uk>
From: Film Insiders <digital@filminsiders.com>
Subject: Virtual screening
Date: 10 December

This message is a reminder that you have claimed a free ticket to an exclusive virtual screening

of *So Then They Walked*. The film becomes available to ------- on our streaming platform at
                                                           139.

6 P.M. GMT on Thursday, 12 December. You ------- four hours to watch the film. Please make sure
                                             140.

the mobile phone number linked to your account is correct so that we can send you an access

code. ------- .
      141.

We are pleased that you are interested in joining us ------- this event. We are excited to share
                                                       142.

this movie with you and hope you enjoy it as much as we do!

TEST 2

139. (A) shows
     (B) actors
     (C) benefits
     (D) viewers

140. (A) had
     (B) will have
     (C) have had
     (D) will be having

141. (A) You can pick up your files any time
         before Thursday.
     (B) Call our customer service department
         to expedite your order.
     (C) You need to enter the code before the
         screening begins.
     (D) Films are a source of entertainment as
         well as information.

142. (A) for
     (B) amid
     (C) upon
     (D) despite

GO ON TO THE NEXT PAGE

Questions 143-146 refer to the following letter.

Dear Scarborough residents,

We want to remind you that the city of Scarborough aims to become an Avian Night Neighborhood. This is a special ------- given to communities that are working to eliminate
143.
unnecessary bright lighting.

You may be wondering why this initiative is ------- . Many birds migrate through this area at
144.
night, and bright lighting can interfere with their navigation.

We can all help by turning off nonessential lights from midnight to 6:00 A.M. ------- . Many shops
145.
have bright floodlights illuminating their storefronts even when they are closed. If you must
have a light on at night, you should direct it downward and away from trees where birds are
likely nesting. ------- , use motion-sensor lights that are on only when absolutely needed.
146.

Thank you!

Diane Slusky
Communications Department
City of Scarborough

143. (A) distinct
(B) distinctive
(C) distinctively
(D) distinction

144. (A) important
(B) familiar
(C) challenging
(D) experimental

145. (A) A trail map is recommended.
(B) We can supply them if needed.
(C) This practice applies to businesses too.
(D) It depends on the particular species.

146. (A) Additionally
(B) Consequently
(C) Nevertheless
(D) Interestingly

PART 7

Directions: In this part you will read a selection of texts, such as magazine and newspaper articles, e-mails, and instant messages. Each text or set of texts is followed by several questions. Select the best answer for each question and mark the letter (A), (B), (C), or (D) on your answer sheet.

Questions 147-148 refer to the following information.

Best Crown Hair Salon
11 Beauty Row
Brisbane
(07) 5550 7990

Name: Madeline Turner

Appointment: 4 August, 11:00 a.m.

Service: Wash, cut, blow-dry

Please notify us at least 24 hours in advance if you need to cancel, or you will be subject to a $25 fee.

---

147. What is the purpose of the information?

(A) To remind a customer about an appointment
(B) To alert patrons to a grand opening
(C) To notify a stylist of a schedule change
(D) To advertise the services available at a salon

148. What detail is included?

(A) A price for a haircut
(B) A business's location
(C) A store owner's name
(D) A customer's phone number

GO ON TO THE NEXT PAGE

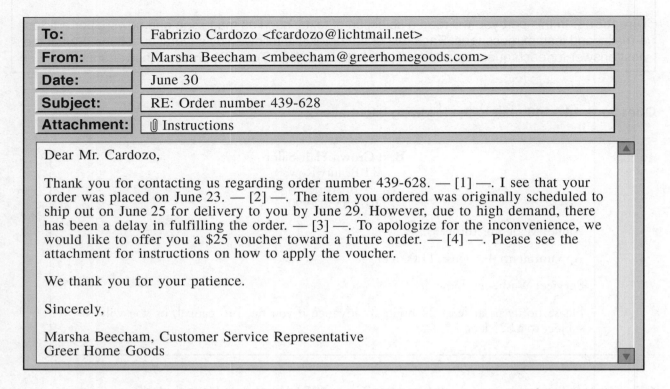

To: Fabrizio Cardozo <fcardozo@lichtmail.net>

From: Marsha Beecham <mbeecham@greerhomegoods.com>

Date: June 30

Subject: RE: Order number 439-628

Attachment: Instructions

Dear Mr. Cardozo,

Thank you for contacting us regarding order number 439-628. — [1] —. I see that your order was placed on June 23. — [2] —. The item you ordered was originally scheduled to ship out on June 25 for delivery to you by June 29. However, due to high demand, there has been a delay in fulfilling the order. — [3] —. To apologize for the inconvenience, we would like to offer you a $25 voucher toward a future order. — [4] —. Please see the attachment for instructions on how to apply the voucher.

We thank you for your patience.

Sincerely,

Marsha Beecham, Customer Service Representative
Greer Home Goods

149. Why did Ms. Beecham send the e-mail?

(A) To respond to an inquiry
(B) To announce a new service
(C) To complain about a late order
(D) To ask that a form be completed

150. What is the topic of the attached instructions?

(A) How to return an order
(B) How to request a refund
(C) How to update an account
(D) How to apply a credit

151. In which of the positions marked [1], [2], [3], and [4] does the following sentence best belong?

"The new expected date of arrival is July 5."

(A) [1]
(B) [2]
(C) [3]
(D) [4]

Questions 152-153 refer to the following article.

Business Briefs

MEXICO CITY (25 June)—When the restaurant Tomoichi Sushi closed last month, Jordan Cohen made a quick decision. He purchased the recently vacated building in the Polanco neighborhood of Mexico City and decided to turn it into a bagel shop.

Mr. Cohen was raised in New York City, where he developed a love for bagels, ring-shaped rolls that are boiled before being baked, resulting in a chewy interior. Bagels are one of the city's most treasured culinary traditions.

The new shop, Lox On Bagels, opened this week. In addition to bagels and spreads, Lox On Bagels serves an assortment of breakfast sandwiches, specialty coffees, and smoothies.

"Bagels were the main staple of my childhood breakfast," Mr. Cohen says. "It's my dream to make them a larger part of Mexican cuisine."

152. According to the article, what is true about Mr. Cohen?
   (A) He works in the construction industry.
   (B) He owns many businesses.
   (C) He was trained as a sushi chef.
   (D) He grew up in New York City.

153. What is indicated about Lox On Bagels?
   (A) It will open at the end of July.
   (B) It has received positive reviews.
   (C) It is in a location that once housed another restaurant.
   (D) It will export bagels to the United States.

GO ON TO THE NEXT PAGE

Questions 154-156 refer to the following letter.

Nakaima Industries
104-1262, Makiku Yoshitsubo
Joetsu-shi, Niigata
Japan

21 November

Kenneth Wallcroft
Wallcroft Pen Designs
2284 Dufferin Street
Marfa, Texas 79843
United States of America

Dear Mr. Wallcroft,

Our board of directors asked me to convey their compliments on your beautifully handcrafted fountain pens. Company President Asa Nakaima, who commissioned the pens to honor our board members, said your work surpassed his expectations. Most noteworthy was how you inscribed the initials of a different board member on each pen. Consequently, every writing implement is a personalized work of art to be cherished.

Mr. Nakaima is also grateful that our company's vice president, Chihiro Hirota, came up with the idea to have you create these gifts, which were distributed at the board's most recent meeting.

Best regards,

Gwen Reger

Gwen Reger, Office Manager
Nakaima Industries

154. What is the purpose of the letter?

(A) To praise an employee
(B) To thank a client for a gift
(C) To express appreciation for an artistic creation
(D) To place an order for promotional items

155. What is mentioned about the pens?

(A) They were manufactured in Japan.
(B) They were presented during an official dinner.
(C) Each contains a different color of ink.
(D) Each includes a unique design feature.

156. What is suggested about Ms. Hirota?

(A) She gift wrapped the pens.
(B) She recommended Mr. Wallcroft's services.
(C) She is in charge of scheduling board meetings.
(D) She signed a contract with Mr. Wallcroft.

Alan Ropp [1:06 P.M.]
Where are you? Weren't we supposed to meet at 1 o'clock to get decorations for the office party?

Camille Saenz [1:07 P.M.]
I'm outside Glinda's Books, the shop next to Parker Fashions.

Alan Ropp [1:08 P.M.]
Oh, OK. I'm in the art supply store. Should I leave and try to find you?

Camille Saenz [1:09 P.M.]
No, don't worry. I know exactly where the art supply store is. I'm walking over now.

Alan Ropp [1:10 P.M.]
Good. They have a roll of bright yellow paper here that we could use to make a banner. It would look very dramatic!

157. Where most likely are Mr. Ropp and Ms. Saenz?

(A) In a theater
(B) In an art museum
(C) In a shopping center
(D) In an office building

158. At 1:09 P.M., what does Ms. Saenz most likely mean when she writes, "No, don't worry"?

(A) She prefers to walk to the office.
(B) She has already made a brightly colored banner.
(C) Mr. Ropp will be reimbursed for any decorations he buys.
(D) Mr. Ropp should stay where he is.

GO ON TO THE NEXT PAGE ▶

Certified Laundry Services

Some health-care facilities believe managing their linen inventory on their premises is practical. However, the costs of handling large volumes of laundry can be high. Allow Certified Laundry Services to supply your sanitized textiles so that you can focus on your core business of patient care. We can schedule weekly or by-request laundry pickup with next-day delivery.

Contact us at 863-555-0119 to arrange a free consultation. We will create a detailed report listing the advantages of using our service, including lowering operating costs. We can compare the actual price-per-pound savings of allowing us to manage your laundry with doing your laundry in-house.

159. For whom is the brochure most likely intended?

(A) Hotels
(B) Hospitals
(C) Beauty salons
(D) Manufacturing companies

160. What is indicated about the report?

(A) It will include client reviews.
(B) It will present new products.
(C) It will describe the region served.
(D) It will provide a cost-savings analysis.

FOR IMMEDIATE RELEASE

Contact: Hiari Mensah, h.mensah@sandarr.com

Sandarr Announces Exciting New Addition to Its Lineup

LOS ANGELES (May 9)—Anyone who has attended a meeting, presentation, or live music concert has most likely seen a Sandarr product in use. As an award-winning designer and producer of microphones and headsets, Sandarr is known for its quality.

Sandarr is pleased to introduce the XTT, a microphone that offers studio-quality sound yet is affordable for the general consumer. For those who work remotely or operate a home-based business, it is essential to have high-quality sound during audio and video conferences so as to be heard clearly by colleagues or clients. Created exclusively for this type of application, the XTT is perfectly suited to all home office environments.

Based on years of research at Sandarr labs, the XTT has been designed to enhance the audio signal quality. The XTT is easily connected to a laptop or desktop computer. The microphone is mounted on a sturdy stand to prevent wobbling.

For further information and pricing, contact Hiari Mensah at h.mensah@sandarr.com or visit www.sandarr.com.

161. What kind of company is Sandarr?

(A) A professional recording studio
(B) A designer of business software
(C) An event management company
(D) A manufacturer of audio equipment

162. According to the press release, who are the intended users of the XTT?

(A) Researchers who record outdoors
(B) Singers who perform live on stage
(C) Announcers who work at radio stations
(D) Workers who join meetings from home

163. The word "mounted" in paragraph 3, line 3, is closest in meaning to

(A) climbed
(B) installed
(C) reached
(D) tested

GO ON TO THE NEXT PAGE

Lonterna Services
www.lonterna.ca

14 January

Audra Bain
Owner, Volta Ten
130 Quillen Street, Suite 265
Toronto, Ontario M5X 1E3

Dear Ms. Bain,

I am pleased to introduce myself as president of Lonterna Services, a Toronto-based social media marketing firm. For the last two years, we have been identified by *Vanguard Monthly* as a leader in social media publicity. Although Lonterna Services was established just four years ago, we have consistently outperformed regional firms that have been in business for over ten years. I am confident that we can help you achieve your marketing goals.

As you know, timing is crucial in your industry, and success often depends on disseminating product information to the public as quickly as possible. Catalogues and flyers may be inexpensive, but they can take weeks to reach potential customers. With a reliable social media team, you can ensure that news about your product will be seen by a large number of people within hours.

Our clients range from fashion retailers to music distributors, but a handful of our team members have deep knowledge of the beverage industry. Their experience ensures that we can start planning a media campaign for you from day one without needing to learn the basics of your business. Please call or e-mail me and let me tell you about the exciting things we can do for you. My direct line is 416-555-0129, and my e-mail address is loh@lonterna.ca.

Sincerely,

Trent Loh

Trent Loh, President

---

164. What most likely does Mr. Loh want Ms. Bain to do?

(A) Subscribe to *Vanguard Monthly*
(B) Hire his company as a contractor
(C) Publish an article about his company
(D) Apply for a marketing job at his company

165. How long has Lonterna Services been in business?

(A) For one year
(B) For two years
(C) For four years
(D) For ten years

166. According to the letter, why is social media marketing so effective?

(A) It reaches the largest number of potential customers.
(B) It delivers information faster than other methods.
(C) It can be easily managed by traditional marketing agencies.
(D) It is less expensive than other methods.

167. What kind of business most likely is Volta Ten?

(A) A fashion retailer
(B) A music distributor
(C) A magazine publisher
(D) A beverage producer

Questions 168-171 refer to the following text-message chain.

Marcus Angelo (6:19 P.M.)
Hi, Geraldo and Claudette. Could one of you bring the box of fabric samples to my apartment on your way home tonight? I forgot it.

Geraldo Soria (6:20 P.M.)
I will. I live around the corner from you. The samples for the HRE Sportswear line?

Marcus Angelo (6:21 P.M.)
Yes. I think I left the box in my office. I'd like to go directly to the client's location tomorrow morning without having to go to the office. It is out of my way.

Geraldo Soria (6:24 P.M.)
I am in your office now. I don't see a box.

Claudette Lymer (6:27 P.M.)
It is in the conference room. I took the samples to show during my video call with the cloth mill's management team.

Marcus Angelo (6:28 P.M.)
Make sure the label reads "HRE Sportswear."

Geraldo Soria (6:30 P.M.)
Got it! You should see me in about 30 minutes.

● ● ●

168. In what type of business do the writers most likely work?

(A) Packaging
(B) Videoconferencing equipment sales
(C) Clothing
(D) Sporting event planning

169. What can be concluded about Mr. Angelo?

(A) He is on vacation.
(B) He is in a meeting.
(C) He has left the office for the day.
(D) He traveled out of town for business.

170. Why did Mr. Soria have trouble finding the box?

(A) Because Mr. Angelo took it home
(B) Because Ms. Lymer had moved it to a new location
(C) Because the clients have it
(D) Because it was sent to the cloth mill managers

171. At 6:30 P.M., what does Mr. Soria most likely mean when he writes, "You should see me in about 30 minutes"?

(A) He will return to the office to see Ms. Lymer.
(B) He will arrive at the client meeting after Ms. Lymer.
(C) He plans to place a video call to Mr. Angelo.
(D) He expects to arrive at Mr. Angelo's apartment soon.

GO ON TO THE NEXT PAGE ➤

To:	Esme MacGregor <emacgregor@hamiltonrealestate.com>
From:	Stockton Office Solutions <sales@stocktonofficesolutions.com>
Date:	March 27
Subject:	Exciting news

Dear Member of the Stockton Office Solutions Family:

Do the responsibilities of your employees require them to sit for long hours at a desk? Do they sometimes feel neck strain, and are their muscles tired and sore at the end of the day? Research shows that being too sedentary can potentially increase the risk of developing health problems. There's one very simple remedy, and that's more movement. — [1] —.

Now there is a great solution: the Stockton Stand-and-Sit Desk. The easily adjustable height of our desk allows workers to alternate between standing and sitting throughout the day without interrupting daily tasks. — [2] —. Now they can move more while never losing productivity. In addition, the Stand-and-Sit Desk also helps improve energy and concentration, which can further enhance productivity. — [3] —.

To upgrade your office work spaces, visit our store today to see three different models of Stand-and-Sit Desks. — [4] —. Because your firm is a regular customer, we are pleased to offer you 25 percent off your purchase of these desks when you order a minimum of five. Visit our online store today at stocktonofficesolutions.com for all your office furniture needs!

172. What is the purpose of the e-mail?

(A) To promote a new product
(B) To offer an employee discount
(C) To request customer feedback
(D) To introduce a new furniture department

173. What is NOT mentioned as a benefit of the Stand-and-Sit desk?

(A) Improved health
(B) Improved group work
(C) Better concentration
(D) Increased productivity

174. What is suggested about Stockton Office Solutions?

(A) It has just opened a new store.
(B) It is currently recruiting sales staff.
(C) It provides free design consultations.
(D) It offers discounts to repeat customers.

175. In which of the positions marked [1], [2], [3], and [4] does the following sentence best belong?

"However, being physically active is not easy when you're in front of a computer all day."

(A) [1]
(B) [2]
(C) [3]
(D) [4]

TEST 2

GO ON TO THE NEXT PAGE

https://www.judithkembeldesigns.ca/home

| **Home** | Gallery | Terms | Contact |

Welcome to my Web site! My name is Judith Kembel, and I am a freelance illustrator in Canada. My career began ten years ago after I completed my degree in art and design. While I have diverse skills, I am known primarily for my artwork featured on mystery novel covers, but I have also been recognised for my nature and wildlife illustrations. I am always open for commissions and can be reached via the e-mail address on my contact page. To facilitate our conversation, please address the following points of information in your e-mail inquiry.

1. A description of your project and personal style preferences

2. Notes about illustrations or design elements that inspire you

3. Confirmation that you have reviewed my contract requirements and understand the rates and payment conditions listed on my Terms page

4. Agreement to a collaborative process that may involve regular communication

To:	Judith Kembel <inquiries@judithkembeldesigns.ca>
From:	Eric Wardza <ewardza@worldmail.ca>
Date:	17 September
Subject:	Commission inquiry

Hello, Ms. Kembel,

I am looking for an artist to design a cover for a book I published several years ago. I would like to release a new edition of the book with updated cover art. Even though people say you can't judge a book by its cover, I read a study stating that 80 percent of people do exactly that. A fresh book cover may help my book capture a new audience.

I envision a fanciful scene with colourful animal characters—something reminiscent of *Speak of the Bees* or *Wisdom of Sea and Sky*, both written by Rufus Wennerstren, for whom you have produced book covers. I have an idea of the style I like and can provide my input as we collaborate on a final design. Please let me know the cost to work with you and whether you have time to work with me.

Best wishes,

Eric Wardza

176. What does Ms. Kembel mention about herself?

(A) She uses the latest design software.
(B) She specializes in a particular type of book.
(C) She teaches design classes occasionally.
(D) She secures most assignments through an agent.

177. What is true about Mr. Wardza's book?

(A) It is the first part of a series.
(B) It has received positive reviews.
(C) It has been published previously.
(D) It is intended for children.

178. Why does Mr. Wardza mention a statistic?

(A) To estimate his book's revenue potential
(B) To offer a reason for wanting to hire Ms. Kembel
(C) To show why he prefers one publisher over another
(D) To propose a new study topic

179. In the e-mail, the word "capture" in paragraph 1, line 4, is closest in meaning to

(A) gain
(B) propose
(C) summarize
(D) represent

180. What point of information does Mr. Wardza fail to include in his message?

(A) Point 1
(B) Point 2
(C) Point 3
(D) Point 4

GO ON TO THE NEXT PAGE

Popular Show to Resume Filming

LONDON (8 July)—Fans of the hit TV series *Best Son* will be treated to a third season—but they will have to wait longer than anticipated to view it.

The drama that centers on the life of Guo Tzeng, the fictitious founder of the Tzeng family business dynasty, debuted two years ago but has gained a sizeable following only in the past year. This delayed jump in viewership prompted top executives at the Roscou streaming platform to approve funding for an additional season, which had been in question.

Because of the six-month gap between filming the previous season and Roscou's late order for the next season, the show has run into scheduling problems with some cast members.

"We discussed trying to rewrite multiple scripts around the characters that would be missing," said Justin Zhou, the award-winning director of *Best Son*. "However, we ultimately decided that doing so would not be true to the story we want to tell."

Many viewers were expecting episodes for season three to become available for viewing in April, the same month previous seasons began. But that timeline is no longer feasible, according to Mr. Zhou. "We will announce a release date soon, but the new episodes probably won't be available until summer at the earliest," he said.

To:	molly.landry@ims.co.uk
From:	lexicotton@ferntreeproductions.co.uk
Date:	17 July
Subject:	Xiao-Ming Hu's availability

Dear Ms. Landry:

I am very relieved that we were able to schedule filming of the third season of *Best Son* for this September and October and that Xiao-Ming Hu will be available then to reprise his role of Guo Tzeng.

I am writing to enquire whether Mr. Hu is available to film the outdoor winter scenes in late December in Churchill, Manitoba. Please let me know as soon as possible, as filming those scenes any sooner might require us to find another location. The shooting of the winter scenes will take about two weeks and will be the last ones scheduled.

Sincerely,

Lexi Cotton
Production Manager, Fern Tree Productions

181. What is the purpose of the article?

(A) To provide an update about a television show
(B) To introduce a new streaming platform
(C) To profile the founder of a family business
(D) To review a popular film series

182. What most likely is Ms. Landry's profession?

(A) Scriptwriter
(B) Talent agent
(C) Set designer
(D) Camera operator

183. When does Ms. Cotton expect filming to be completed?

(A) In April
(B) In June
(C) In August
(D) In December

184. What is most likely true about Fern Tree Productions?

(A) It is owned by Mr. Zhou.
(B) It specializes in documentaries.
(C) It received funding from Roscou.
(D) It has reduced its operating budget.

185. What can be concluded about Mr. Hu?

(A) He enjoys winter sports.
(B) He owns a home in Churchill.
(C) He is unavailable in September.
(D) He plays a leading role in *Best Son*.

GO ON TO THE NEXT PAGE

Dovmart Executive Meeting Agenda

Location: Room 404, Billings Building

Date: April 30

Time: 10:00 A.M.

Agenda Item

Dovmart is concerned about delays in getting goods, including grocery products, into the hands of our customers. Store managers are frustrated, and customers are complaining. To resolve this issue, we will discuss proposals for solutions from our operations team.

Proposal 1: Extend store hours while considering costs and staffing needs (Donald Toye).

Proposal 2: Train employees to become delivery drivers (Jimeana Moreano).

Proposal 3: Open new warehouse locations (Jacob Gaburo).

Proposal 4: Establish relationships with new suppliers (Satoshi Yamada).

Attention, Dovmart Employees

May 10

We are offering a twelve-week program to train Dovmart supply-chain employees to become certified long-haul truck drivers by September 1. Participants will learn how to operate company-owned tractor-trailer trucks. They will also prepare for the written and practical portions of the commercial driver's license test.

What are the advantages of becoming a long-distance trucker?

• Learn a skill that is in high demand.

• Enjoy flexible scheduling.

• Earn a substantially higher salary.

Long-distance truck drivers will drive to and from Dovmart warehouses and retail locations. Drivers choose between regional and cross-country routes. To learn more, log on to the Dovmart internal Web site and follow the program link. Enroll before May 15 to receive a bonus.

Joe Radovich [12:13 P.M.]
Hello, Amelie. I'm almost finished with the training program. I can't wait to get my commercial driver's license.

Amelie Ziff [12:15 P.M.]
I'm sure you will be terrific in your new position, but I will miss having you on my team. You were one of the top supply-chain associates at our store here in Madison.

Joe Radovich [12:16 P.M.]
I will miss my job, too, but the program sounded too interesting to pass up. I even received a bonus when I joined! My last day in Madison will be August 30.

186. According to the agenda, what aspect of Dovmart products concerns customers?

(A) Their prices
(B) Their quality
(C) Their ingredients
(D) Their availability

187. Whose proposal did company executives share with employees on May 10?

(A) Mr. Toye's
(B) Ms. Moreano's
(C) Mr. Gaburo's
(D) Mr. Yamada's

188. What does the notice indicate about employees who complete the program?

(A) They will have opportunities to work overtime.
(B) They will need to take courses every year.
(C) They will earn more money.
(D) They will work overseas.

189. What does the notice instruct interested employees to do?

(A) Sign up for a test
(B) Consult a schedule
(C) Visit the company's Web site
(D) Submit preferences for routes

190. What is most likely true about Mr. Radovich?

(A) He already has a commercial driver's license.
(B) He enrolled in a training program before May 15.
(C) He will begin a new job in Madison soon.
(D) He hired Ms. Ziff as a supply-chain associate.

GO ON TO THE NEXT PAGE

Brea Autolot
58 Dahill Street
Hamilton, Virginia 20158

Sales for Model TX-400, Quarter 1

Exterior Color (by popularity)	Percentage of Total Sales
White	32%
Black	26%
Gray	15%
Blue	10%
Silver	9%
Other (Red, Green, Beige)	8%

Projections for quarter 2: Similar patterns. Blue is the only color Brea Autolot expects to increase in sales in the second quarter. Beginning in quarter 2, model TX-400 will also be available in bronze.

To:	Rhea Adams <radams@breaautolot.com>
From:	Anna Watkins <awatkins@mailcrate.com>
Date:	September 9
Subject:	Car purchase

Dear Ms. Adams,

Thank you for taking the time to show me so many sport utility vehicles at Brea Autolot this week. I appreciated working with you, so I wanted you to know why I decided to go elsewhere for the car I purchased. Your dealership had an abundance of model TX-400s but none with all the extra features that I was looking for. Makefield Auto had the model TX-400 in the silver color I wanted with those features.

In addition, my father is a member of the Makefield Auto rewards program, and he referred me to that dealership. He was able to transfer all of his 10,000 rewards points to me, enabling me to reduce substantially the purchase price of my model TX-400. You are an excellent salesperson; it is just that I found a better deal with another dealership.

Sincerely,

Anna Watkins

MAKEFIELD AUTO

Model TX-400—The Top-Rated Sport Utility Vehicle (SUV) of the Year

This year's eight-passenger model includes more passenger space and a more comfortable ride with lots of second-row legroom and an expanded third row.

- Rear-seat media system for the first time includes touch screens for second-row passengers.
- The built-in exterior cameras offer nine available views.
- The safety system alerts you when it detects a pedestrian directly in front of your vehicle.
- The model TX-400 gets the best gas mileage of any car in its size category.

Join the Makefield Auto rewards program when you buy a vehicle. Every time you visit our dealership for a service or to purchase a car, you will be rewarded with points that can be redeemed on a purchase or service. As a bonus, you will earn 100 rewards points each time you refer someone to our dealership.

---

191. What does the report suggest Brea Autolot will do in quarter 2?

(A) Open a second location
(B) Sell more blue model TX-400s
(C) Improve staff training
(D) Stop selling the bronze model TX-400

192. What can be concluded about the color of the TX-400 that Ms. Watkins purchased?

(A) It is expected to be Makefield Auto's best-selling color TX-400 in quarter 2.
(B) That color is no longer available from the manufacturer.
(C) In quarter 1, 9 percent of Brea Autolot's sales of TX-400s were that color.
(D) The manufacturer usually sells 10,000 units in that color.

193. What is a reason Ms. Watkins gives for purchasing a car from Makefield Auto?

(A) The extra features
(B) The excellent sales help
(C) The wide variety of colors
(D) The home-delivery service

194. What can be concluded about Ms. Watkins' father?

(A) He received 100 bonus points.
(B) He recently bought a car from Brea Autolot.
(C) He owns a green model TX-400.
(D) He transferred his vehicle ownership to Ms. Watkins.

195. According to the advertisement, what is new in this year's model TX-400?

(A) The superior fuel efficiency
(B) The built-in exterior cameras
(C) The touch screens for passengers
(D) The pedestrian-alert safety system

GO ON TO THE NEXT PAGE ➡

To:	Sarah Abboud <sabboud@mailhost.co.uk>
From:	Eun-Mi Yoon <emyoon@opalmail.co.uk>
Date:	8 February
Subject:	Lecture series

Hi Sarah,

I hope you are settled into your new job. We miss you around the office. I thought you might be interested in the upcoming lecture series from Travel the World Society (TTWS). It would be fun to attend one of the lectures together, since they are interactive and participants might be able to turn on their cameras at some point. I attended a great one last year. To view the speaker lineup, visit www.ttws.org/events. I prefer the March lecture, but the April and May topics also look good. I am a member of TTWS. You don't have to join to buy a ticket, but you will get a discount if you do.

Eun-Mi

---

https://www.ttws.org/events

Home	**Events**	Blogs	Membership

LECTURE SERIES

Travel the World Society (TTWS) is pleased to announce that tickets for its fifth annual lecture series are now on sale. Tickets for the virtual lectures are £25 each or £95 for all four.* Each lecture starts at noon GMT and lasts 90 minutes. The final 15 minutes are reserved for an open exchange among the speakers and participants.

- *15 March* — **Ashraf Shirvani**, professor of Iranian culture, discusses traditional clothing and textiles of ancient Persia.
- *22 April* — **Carolina Perez**, art historian, explores sculpture through Mexico's most important statues.
- *28 May* (SOLD OUT) — **Marcel Bisset**, five-star chef, explores the culinary delights of France's Normandy region.
- *12 June* — **Aoki Watanabe**, host of the hit travel TV show *Let's Tour Japan*, shares the sights and sounds of Japan's island of Kyushu.

A link will be e-mailed to ticket holders five days prior to each event.

*TTWS members pay £20 for an individual ticket or £75 for all four. Simply include your membership number on the order form to get your discount. To join TTWS, visit the Membership page.

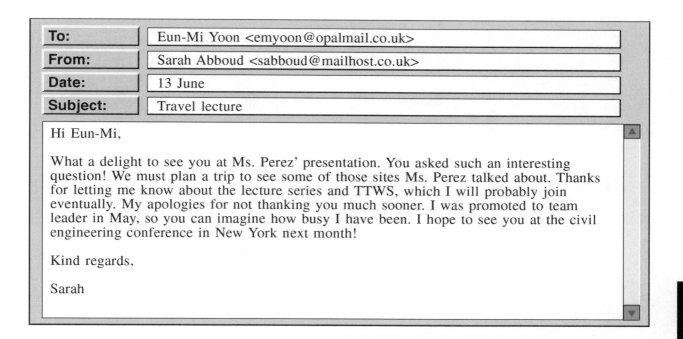

To:	Eun-Mi Yoon <emyoon@opalmail.co.uk>
From:	Sarah Abboud <sabboud@mailhost.co.uk>
Date:	13 June
Subject:	Travel lecture

Hi Eun-Mi,

What a delight to see you at Ms. Perez' presentation. You asked such an interesting question! We must plan a trip to see some of those sites Ms. Perez talked about. Thanks for letting me know about the lecture series and TTWS, which I will probably join eventually. My apologies for not thanking you much sooner. I was promoted to team leader in May, so you can imagine how busy I have been. I hope to see you at the civil engineering conference in New York next month!

Kind regards,

Sarah

196. What does the first e-mail suggest about Ms. Yoon?

(A) She formerly worked with Ms. Abboud.
(B) She recently changed jobs.
(C) She is going to Japan in June.
(D) She has never attended a TTWS event.

197. What does the Web page indicate about the lecture series?

(A) It is presented online only.
(B) It took place for the first time last year.
(C) Its speakers lead guided tours.
(D) Its most popular speaker is Mr. Watanabe.

198. What is true about Ms. Abboud?

(A) She will lead a workshop at an engineering conference.
(B) She is a top executive at her company.
(C) She paid £25 for a lecture ticket.
(D) She arrived fifteen minutes late to an event.

199. What is the topic of the lecture attended by Ms. Yoon and Ms. Abboud?

(A) Clothes and textiles
(B) Sculpture and statues
(C) French food
(D) Japanese islands

200. In the second e-mail, what does Ms. Abboud suggest that she and Ms. Yoon do?

(A) Discuss a question from the TTWS blog
(B) Book rooms in the same hotel
(C) Join a professional organization
(D) Visit some sites that they learned about

Stop! This is the end of the test. If you finish before time is called, you may go back to Parts 5, 6, and 7 and check your work.

公式 TOEIC® Listening & Reading 問題集 11

2024 年 7 月 19 日　第 1 版 第 1 刷発行
2024 年 9 月 5 日　第 1 版 第 2 刷発行

著者	ETS
編集協力	株式会社 カルチャー・プロ
	株式会社 WIT HOUSE
発行元	一般財団法人 国際ビジネスコミュニケーション協会
	〒 100-0014
	東京都千代田区永田町 2-14-2
	山王グランドビル
	電話　050-1790-7410
印刷	大日本印刷株式会社

TEST 1

解答用紙

REGISTRATION No.
受験番号

フリガナ

NAME
氏名

LISTENING SECTION

Part 1

No.	ANSWER A B C D
1	Ⓐ Ⓑ Ⓒ Ⓓ
2	Ⓐ Ⓑ Ⓒ Ⓓ
3	Ⓐ Ⓑ Ⓒ Ⓓ
4	Ⓐ Ⓑ Ⓒ Ⓓ
5	Ⓐ Ⓑ Ⓒ Ⓓ
6	Ⓐ Ⓑ Ⓒ Ⓓ
7	Ⓐ Ⓑ Ⓒ Ⓓ
8	Ⓐ Ⓑ Ⓒ Ⓓ
9	Ⓐ Ⓑ Ⓒ Ⓓ
10	Ⓐ Ⓑ Ⓒ Ⓓ

Part 2

No.	ANSWER A B C
11	Ⓐ Ⓑ Ⓒ
12	Ⓐ Ⓑ Ⓒ
13	Ⓐ Ⓑ Ⓒ
14	Ⓐ Ⓑ Ⓒ
15	Ⓐ Ⓑ Ⓒ
16	Ⓐ Ⓑ Ⓒ
17	Ⓐ Ⓑ Ⓒ
18	Ⓐ Ⓑ Ⓒ
19	Ⓐ Ⓑ Ⓒ
20	Ⓐ Ⓑ Ⓒ

No.	ANSWER A B C
21	Ⓐ Ⓑ Ⓒ
22	Ⓐ Ⓑ Ⓒ
23	Ⓐ Ⓑ Ⓒ
24	Ⓐ Ⓑ Ⓒ
25	Ⓐ Ⓑ Ⓒ
26	Ⓐ Ⓑ Ⓒ
27	Ⓐ Ⓑ Ⓒ
28	Ⓐ Ⓑ Ⓒ
29	Ⓐ Ⓑ Ⓒ
30	Ⓐ Ⓑ Ⓒ

Part 3

No.	ANSWER A B C D
31	Ⓐ Ⓑ Ⓒ Ⓓ
32	Ⓐ Ⓑ Ⓒ Ⓓ
33	Ⓐ Ⓑ Ⓒ Ⓓ
34	Ⓐ Ⓑ Ⓒ Ⓓ
35	Ⓐ Ⓑ Ⓒ Ⓓ
36	Ⓐ Ⓑ Ⓒ Ⓓ
37	Ⓐ Ⓑ Ⓒ Ⓓ
38	Ⓐ Ⓑ Ⓒ Ⓓ
39	Ⓐ Ⓑ Ⓒ Ⓓ
40	Ⓐ Ⓑ Ⓒ Ⓓ
41	Ⓐ Ⓑ Ⓒ Ⓓ
42	Ⓐ Ⓑ Ⓒ Ⓓ
43	Ⓐ Ⓑ Ⓒ Ⓓ
44	Ⓐ Ⓑ Ⓒ Ⓓ
45	Ⓐ Ⓑ Ⓒ Ⓓ
46	Ⓐ Ⓑ Ⓒ Ⓓ
47	Ⓐ Ⓑ Ⓒ Ⓓ
48	Ⓐ Ⓑ Ⓒ Ⓓ
49	Ⓐ Ⓑ Ⓒ Ⓓ
50	Ⓐ Ⓑ Ⓒ Ⓓ
51	Ⓐ Ⓑ Ⓒ Ⓓ
52	Ⓐ Ⓑ Ⓒ Ⓓ
53	Ⓐ Ⓑ Ⓒ Ⓓ
54	Ⓐ Ⓑ Ⓒ Ⓓ
55	Ⓐ Ⓑ Ⓒ Ⓓ
56	Ⓐ Ⓑ Ⓒ Ⓓ
57	Ⓐ Ⓑ Ⓒ Ⓓ
58	Ⓐ Ⓑ Ⓒ Ⓓ
59	Ⓐ Ⓑ Ⓒ Ⓓ
60	Ⓐ Ⓑ Ⓒ Ⓓ
61	Ⓐ Ⓑ Ⓒ Ⓓ
62	Ⓐ Ⓑ Ⓒ Ⓓ
63	Ⓐ Ⓑ Ⓒ Ⓓ
64	Ⓐ Ⓑ Ⓒ Ⓓ
65	Ⓐ Ⓑ Ⓒ Ⓓ
66	Ⓐ Ⓑ Ⓒ Ⓓ
67	Ⓐ Ⓑ Ⓒ Ⓓ
68	Ⓐ Ⓑ Ⓒ Ⓓ
69	Ⓐ Ⓑ Ⓒ Ⓓ
70	Ⓐ Ⓑ Ⓒ Ⓓ

Part 4

No.	ANSWER A B C D
71	Ⓐ Ⓑ Ⓒ Ⓓ
72	Ⓐ Ⓑ Ⓒ Ⓓ
73	Ⓐ Ⓑ Ⓒ Ⓓ
74	Ⓐ Ⓑ Ⓒ Ⓓ
75	Ⓐ Ⓑ Ⓒ Ⓓ
76	Ⓐ Ⓑ Ⓒ Ⓓ
77	Ⓐ Ⓑ Ⓒ Ⓓ
78	Ⓐ Ⓑ Ⓒ Ⓓ
79	Ⓐ Ⓑ Ⓒ Ⓓ
80	Ⓐ Ⓑ Ⓒ Ⓓ
81	Ⓐ Ⓑ Ⓒ Ⓓ
82	Ⓐ Ⓑ Ⓒ Ⓓ
83	Ⓐ Ⓑ Ⓒ Ⓓ
84	Ⓐ Ⓑ Ⓒ Ⓓ
85	Ⓐ Ⓑ Ⓒ Ⓓ
86	Ⓐ Ⓑ Ⓒ Ⓓ
87	Ⓐ Ⓑ Ⓒ Ⓓ
88	Ⓐ Ⓑ Ⓒ Ⓓ
89	Ⓐ Ⓑ Ⓒ Ⓓ
90	Ⓐ Ⓑ Ⓒ Ⓓ
91	Ⓐ Ⓑ Ⓒ Ⓓ
92	Ⓐ Ⓑ Ⓒ Ⓓ
93	Ⓐ Ⓑ Ⓒ Ⓓ
94	Ⓐ Ⓑ Ⓒ Ⓓ
95	Ⓐ Ⓑ Ⓒ Ⓓ
96	Ⓐ Ⓑ Ⓒ Ⓓ
97	Ⓐ Ⓑ Ⓒ Ⓓ
98	Ⓐ Ⓑ Ⓒ Ⓓ
99	Ⓐ Ⓑ Ⓒ Ⓓ
100	Ⓐ Ⓑ Ⓒ Ⓓ

READING SECTION

Part 5

No.	ANSWER A B C D
101	Ⓐ Ⓑ Ⓒ Ⓓ
102	Ⓐ Ⓑ Ⓒ Ⓓ
103	Ⓐ Ⓑ Ⓒ Ⓓ
104	Ⓐ Ⓑ Ⓒ Ⓓ
105	Ⓐ Ⓑ Ⓒ Ⓓ
106	Ⓐ Ⓑ Ⓒ Ⓓ
107	Ⓐ Ⓑ Ⓒ Ⓓ
108	Ⓐ Ⓑ Ⓒ Ⓓ
109	Ⓐ Ⓑ Ⓒ Ⓓ
110	Ⓐ Ⓑ Ⓒ Ⓓ
111	Ⓐ Ⓑ Ⓒ Ⓓ
112	Ⓐ Ⓑ Ⓒ Ⓓ
113	Ⓐ Ⓑ Ⓒ Ⓓ
114	Ⓐ Ⓑ Ⓒ Ⓓ
115	Ⓐ Ⓑ Ⓒ Ⓓ
116	Ⓐ Ⓑ Ⓒ Ⓓ
117	Ⓐ Ⓑ Ⓒ Ⓓ
118	Ⓐ Ⓑ Ⓒ Ⓓ
119	Ⓐ Ⓑ Ⓒ Ⓓ
120	Ⓐ Ⓑ Ⓒ Ⓓ

Part 6

No.	ANSWER A B C D
121	Ⓐ Ⓑ Ⓒ Ⓓ
122	Ⓐ Ⓑ Ⓒ Ⓓ
123	Ⓐ Ⓑ Ⓒ Ⓓ
124	Ⓐ Ⓑ Ⓒ Ⓓ
125	Ⓐ Ⓑ Ⓒ Ⓓ
126	Ⓐ Ⓑ Ⓒ Ⓓ
127	Ⓐ Ⓑ Ⓒ Ⓓ
128	Ⓐ Ⓑ Ⓒ Ⓓ
129	Ⓐ Ⓑ Ⓒ Ⓓ
130	Ⓐ Ⓑ Ⓒ Ⓓ
131	Ⓐ Ⓑ Ⓒ Ⓓ
132	Ⓐ Ⓑ Ⓒ Ⓓ
133	Ⓐ Ⓑ Ⓒ Ⓓ
134	Ⓐ Ⓑ Ⓒ Ⓓ
135	Ⓐ Ⓑ Ⓒ Ⓓ
136	Ⓐ Ⓑ Ⓒ Ⓓ
137	Ⓐ Ⓑ Ⓒ Ⓓ
138	Ⓐ Ⓑ Ⓒ Ⓓ
139	Ⓐ Ⓑ Ⓒ Ⓓ
140	Ⓐ Ⓑ Ⓒ Ⓓ

Part 7

No.	ANSWER A B C D
141	Ⓐ Ⓑ Ⓒ Ⓓ
142	Ⓐ Ⓑ Ⓒ Ⓓ
143	Ⓐ Ⓑ Ⓒ Ⓓ
144	Ⓐ Ⓑ Ⓒ Ⓓ
145	Ⓐ Ⓑ Ⓒ Ⓓ
146	Ⓐ Ⓑ Ⓒ Ⓓ
147	Ⓐ Ⓑ Ⓒ Ⓓ
148	Ⓐ Ⓑ Ⓒ Ⓓ
149	Ⓐ Ⓑ Ⓒ Ⓓ
150	Ⓐ Ⓑ Ⓒ Ⓓ
151	Ⓐ Ⓑ Ⓒ Ⓓ
152	Ⓐ Ⓑ Ⓒ Ⓓ
153	Ⓐ Ⓑ Ⓒ Ⓓ
154	Ⓐ Ⓑ Ⓒ Ⓓ
155	Ⓐ Ⓑ Ⓒ Ⓓ
156	Ⓐ Ⓑ Ⓒ Ⓓ
157	Ⓐ Ⓑ Ⓒ Ⓓ
158	Ⓐ Ⓑ Ⓒ Ⓓ
159	Ⓐ Ⓑ Ⓒ Ⓓ
160	Ⓐ Ⓑ Ⓒ Ⓓ
161	Ⓐ Ⓑ Ⓒ Ⓓ
162	Ⓐ Ⓑ Ⓒ Ⓓ
163	Ⓐ Ⓑ Ⓒ Ⓓ
164	Ⓐ Ⓑ Ⓒ Ⓓ
165	Ⓐ Ⓑ Ⓒ Ⓓ
166	Ⓐ Ⓑ Ⓒ Ⓓ
167	Ⓐ Ⓑ Ⓒ Ⓓ
168	Ⓐ Ⓑ Ⓒ Ⓓ
169	Ⓐ Ⓑ Ⓒ Ⓓ
170	Ⓐ Ⓑ Ⓒ Ⓓ
171	Ⓐ Ⓑ Ⓒ Ⓓ
172	Ⓐ Ⓑ Ⓒ Ⓓ
173	Ⓐ Ⓑ Ⓒ Ⓓ
174	Ⓐ Ⓑ Ⓒ Ⓓ
175	Ⓐ Ⓑ Ⓒ Ⓓ
176	Ⓐ Ⓑ Ⓒ Ⓓ
177	Ⓐ Ⓑ Ⓒ Ⓓ
178	Ⓐ Ⓑ Ⓒ Ⓓ
179	Ⓐ Ⓑ Ⓒ Ⓓ
180	Ⓐ Ⓑ Ⓒ Ⓓ
181	Ⓐ Ⓑ Ⓒ Ⓓ
182	Ⓐ Ⓑ Ⓒ Ⓓ
183	Ⓐ Ⓑ Ⓒ Ⓓ
184	Ⓐ Ⓑ Ⓒ Ⓓ
185	Ⓐ Ⓑ Ⓒ Ⓓ
186	Ⓐ Ⓑ Ⓒ Ⓓ
187	Ⓐ Ⓑ Ⓒ Ⓓ
188	Ⓐ Ⓑ Ⓒ Ⓓ
189	Ⓐ Ⓑ Ⓒ Ⓓ
190	Ⓐ Ⓑ Ⓒ Ⓓ
191	Ⓐ Ⓑ Ⓒ Ⓓ
192	Ⓐ Ⓑ Ⓒ Ⓓ
193	Ⓐ Ⓑ Ⓒ Ⓓ
194	Ⓐ Ⓑ Ⓒ Ⓓ
195	Ⓐ Ⓑ Ⓒ Ⓓ
196	Ⓐ Ⓑ Ⓒ Ⓓ
197	Ⓐ Ⓑ Ⓒ Ⓓ
198	Ⓐ Ⓑ Ⓒ Ⓓ
199	Ⓐ Ⓑ Ⓒ Ⓓ
200	Ⓐ Ⓑ Ⓒ Ⓓ

TEST 2

解答用紙

REGISTRATION No.
受験番号

フリガナ

NAME
氏名

LISTENING SECTION

Part 1

No.	ANSWER A B C D
1	A B C D
2	A B C D
3	A B C D
4	A B C D
5	A B C D
6	A B C D
7	A B C D
8	A B C D
9	A B C D
10	A B C D

Part 2

No.	ANSWER A B C
11	A B C
12	A B C
13	A B C
14	A B C
15	A B C
16	A B C
17	A B C
18	A B C
19	A B C
20	A B C

No.	ANSWER A B C
21	A B C
22	A B C
23	A B C
24	A B C
25	A B C
26	A B C
27	A B C
28	A B C
29	A B C
30	A B C

Part 3

No.	ANSWER A B C D
31	A B C D
32	A B C D
33	A B C D
34	A B C D
35	A B C D
36	A B C D
37	A B C D
38	A B C D
39	A B C D
40	A B C D

No.	ANSWER A B C D
41	A B C D
42	A B C D
43	A B C D
44	A B C D
45	A B C D
46	A B C D
47	A B C D
48	A B C D
49	A B C D
50	A B C D

No.	ANSWER A B C D
51	A B C D
52	A B C D
53	A B C D
54	A B C D
55	A B C D
56	A B C D
57	A B C D
58	A B C D
59	A B C D
60	A B C D

Part 4

No.	ANSWER A B C D
61	A B C D
62	A B C D
63	A B C D
64	A B C D
65	A B C D
66	A B C D
67	A B C D
68	A B C D
69	A B C D
70	A B C D

No.	ANSWER A B C D
71	A B C D
72	A B C D
73	A B C D
74	A B C D
75	A B C D
76	A B C D
77	A B C D
78	A B C D
79	A B C D
80	A B C D

No.	ANSWER A B C D
81	A B C D
82	A B C D
83	A B C D
84	A B C D
85	A B C D
86	A B C D
87	A B C D
88	A B C D
89	A B C D
90	A B C D

No.	ANSWER A B C D
91	A B C D
92	A B C D
93	A B C D
94	A B C D
95	A B C D
96	A B C D
97	A B C D
98	A B C D
99	A B C D
100	A B C D

READING SECTION

Part 5

No.	ANSWER A B C D
101	A B C D
102	A B C D
103	A B C D
104	A B C D
105	A B C D
106	A B C D
107	A B C D
108	A B C D
109	A B C D
110	A B C D

No.	ANSWER A B C D
111	A B C D
112	A B C D
113	A B C D
114	A B C D
115	A B C D
116	A B C D
117	A B C D
118	A B C D
119	A B C D
120	A B C D

Part 6

No.	ANSWER A B C D
121	A B C D
122	A B C D
123	A B C D
124	A B C D
125	A B C D
126	A B C D
127	A B C D
128	A B C D
129	A B C D
130	A B C D

No.	ANSWER A B C D
131	A B C D
132	A B C D
133	A B C D
134	A B C D
135	A B C D
136	A B C D
137	A B C D
138	A B C D
139	A B C D
140	A B C D

Part 7

No.	ANSWER A B C D
141	A B C D
142	A B C D
143	A B C D
144	A B C D
145	A B C D
146	A B C D
147	A B C D
148	A B C D
149	A B C D
150	A B C D

No.	ANSWER A B C D
151	A B C D
152	A B C D
153	A B C D
154	A B C D
155	A B C D
156	A B C D
157	A B C D
158	A B C D
159	A B C D
160	A B C D

No.	ANSWER A B C D
161	A B C D
162	A B C D
163	A B C D
164	A B C D
165	A B C D
166	A B C D
167	A B C D
168	A B C D
169	A B C D
170	A B C D

No.	ANSWER A B C D
171	A B C D
172	A B C D
173	A B C D
174	A B C D
175	A B C D
176	A B C D
177	A B C D
178	A B C D
179	A B C D
180	A B C D

No.	ANSWER A B C D
181	A B C D
182	A B C D
183	A B C D
184	A B C D
185	A B C D
186	A B C D
187	A B C D
188	A B C D
189	A B C D
190	A B C D

No.	ANSWER A B C D
191	A B C D
192	A B C D
193	A B C D
194	A B C D
195	A B C D
196	A B C D
197	A B C D
198	A B C D
199	A B C D
200	A B C D